Phil Whyman's
Dead Haunted

Phil Whyman's
Dead Haunted

Paranormal Encounters and Investigations

NEW HOLLAND

First published in 2007 by New Holland Publishers (UK) Ltd
London • Cape Town • Sydney • Auckland
www.newhollandpublishers.com

Garfield House, 86–88 Edgware Road,
London W2 2EA, United Kingdom
80 McKenzie Street, Cape Town 8001, South Africa
14 Aquatic Drive, Frenchs Forest, NSW 2086, Australia
218 Lake Road, Northcote, Auckland, New Zealand

10 9 8 7 6 5 4 3 2 1

ISBN: 978 1 84537 536 2

Editorial Director: Jo Hemmings
Project Editor: Gareth Jones
Copy Editor: Sarah Larter
Designer: Gülen Shevki-Taylor
Production: Joan Woodroffe
Indexer: Angie Hipkin

Reproduction by Pica Digital Pte Ltd, Singapore
Printed and bound by Kyodo Printing Co (Singapore) Pte Ltd

Contents

INTRODUCTION

Ghosts ... What exactly are they and where do they come from? Well, let me clear up the first part of that question by simply saying that nobody really knows exactly what they are – and those who tell you they do know what they are would probably boast about knowing the meaning of life too! As for the second part of that question – well, that's an even bigger mystery, which we'll take a look at a little later.

Ghosts seem to have been around for ages – certainly hundreds and maybe even thousands of years. Since humans started to record their lives, events have been documented that tell of strange, ghostly encounters, which people simply cannot explain.

Before we go any further, let me spark your imagination a little. Picture this scene:

You're spending the evening with friends, chatting and having a drink when the conversation turns to the subject of ghosts and haunted houses. Eventually, after much story telling and debate, the time comes for you to leave.

As you start the long walk home you suddenly realize that it's extremely dark, the wind is picking up and there's not a soul in sight. This is when it dawns on you – you have to walk past the local church, complete with its ancient, gloomy graveyard. Your stride quickens as you draw level with the church, and you try not to look at the graves – it's then that you suddenly catch a glimpse of 'It'!

Standing at the side of one of the headstones is a tall, dark, hooded figure with red, glowing eyes. You try to ignore the scene and pass it off as a figment of your overactive imagination, but it's too late – it knows you have seen it and starts to move. With your heart almost pounding out of your chest you respond and start to run in panic, tripping as you do so. Now 'It' is standing over you and from its hooded robe slowly extends a bony, claw-like hand. It's getting closer and closer, the bony hand almost at your throat, when suddenly...

And I'll stop there, because, of course, what I've just recounted is complete and utter nonsense!

Believe it or not, thanks to television, cinema and horror novels, the above scenario is what many people imagine an encounter with a ghost will be like. And while we're at it, just what is the fascination about giving all things paranormal and ghostly red, glowing eyes? I've never been able to fathom that one out. Well, I'm sorry to disappoint you all, but it is just not like that. In fact on most occasions people don't actually realize what's happening when they see a ghost!

'Why?', I hear you ask? Surely something that looks like a levitating bedsheet or has the same characteristics as an oversized, green bogey can't be all that difficult to suss out – or can it? Well, the truth is that nearly all ghost sightings actually look like things we see in everyday life. For example, ghosts of people seem quite normal, as do ghosts of animals. It's not until something totally unexpected and weird happens that we question what we have just seen. This usually takes the form of the ghost's favourite party trick, which is to vanish in front of our eyes!

Seriously though, the subject of the paranormal and ghosts in particular is a long and exhausting road along which to travel, so let me be your guide as we take a look into this intriguing and often thought-provoking world.

Our first port of call on our journey into the realm of the unexplained is to give you an insight into the what, why and when I was first hooked on all things ghostly – namely my first paranormal experience. So, here, in all its glory, is an account of that very experience, which occurred when I was about 15 years old.

I have a very good memory – in certain instances it seems almost photographic – so I am able to recall the event like it happened yesterday. One sunny afternoon I was sitting in my bedroom at my keyboard, plugging away at one of my compositions for a music exam, which was fast approaching. I was positioned with my back to my bedroom window and immediately in front of me, about 8 feet away, was my bedroom door. My bed was against a wall to the left of me. The door opened onto the upstairs landing and on this occasion it was ajar, affording me a view of part of the house.

OPPOSITE: *Paranormal encounters rarely, if ever, involve the sort of ghostly figures that have become a staple of horror novels and films.*

Anyway, I was happily playing my keyboard, when I happened to take my gaze off the black and white keys and look out of my bedroom door. As I did so my eyes were met with a sight that did not quite register fully, for a few seconds at least. A medium-sized ginger cat had just walked past my door from right to left. Nothing strange about that you may think. Indeed, nothing strange about that at all – until you realize, as I did a few seconds after the event, that the only ginger cat we had had in the Whyman household had died some months before.

Mitzie, as he was known, was a very friendly fellow and was the favourite pet of my mother. Every night he would either sleep on my parents' bed or at the bottom of my bed, after doing his usual routine of 'kneading' the duvet with his paws in an effort to form a cosy spot on which to snooze, an experience that is no doubt familiar with any cat owners reading this.

One day, while my parents were on holiday and I was house-sitting, Mitzie came into the house late at night with a mouse. Despite my best efforts to liberate the rodent from the cat's jaws, Mitzie escaped back outside through a window that was left open for him to come and go as he pleased. Rather annoyed, I went to bed.

At about 9.30 am the next morning there was a knock at the front door. As I opened it, I was somewhat surprised to see one of my neighbours standing there on the path. They quietly asked me if I had a ginger cat, to which I answered in the affirmative. I was devastated to hear that Mitzie had been found dead close to their house, having apparently been struck by a vehicle of some kind during the night. I fetched him, gently lowered him into the ground of my parents' back garden and said a few final words.

As Mitzie was the only ginger cat we had at that time I can only assume that he had somehow come back to pay us a visit. But that may not be the only time he has visited. To this day when my parents are lying in bed, my mother often feels what she describes as a 'small animal' jump onto the bed, walk around a little before lying down and then gently disappear. And, what's more, the same thing has happened to me in my bedroom in that house on several occasions – but it has never worried or alarmed me.

And that is my very first paranormal experience as I remember it. I often look back at that night when Mitzie had the mouse, as I know that if I had taken the mouse off him I would have kept the cat in the house until the following morning, a thought that still saddens me today.

Now, let's move on to the first chapter...

LEFT: *Graveyards have long been associated with ghosts and spirits, although it may be a common misconception that they are the best locations to look for them.*

ABOVE: *Mitzie, the family cat, who I believe I saw when I was about 14–15 years of age, after he had died as a result of a tragic road accident.*

I

Ghosts and Their Attributes

Okay, so let us begin this journey by looking at the various types of ghosts. 'Uh, various types?' I hear you ask. Well yes… It's a common misconception that there is just one type of ghost, and the image that normally springs to mind is that of a figure dressed in the clothes of a bygone age who walks through walls. And, while this kind of apparition does occur, it is by no means the only kind of ghost you can encounter. Oh, and it's worth noting that a ghost doesn't actually have to appear – or manifest itself, as this is properly known – at all!

For those of you who are new to the subject of ghosts, I'll give a brief and simple explanation of what's what. Here we go…

In all the situations where there is believed to be ghostly activity or paranormal phenomena, the event is generally regarded as a haunting and places where such activity occurs can be described as haunted. Incidentally, the term 'paranormal', which dates from the early 1900s, is used as a label for something that cannot be explained scientifically.

So now that's been cleared up, we'll move on to some of the different types of ghosts…

RESIDUAL HAUNTINGS

Residual hauntings are rather strange affairs in that most paranormal investigators don't actually class them as true ghosts. However, it is believed that this type of event makes up a high percentage of sightings! Now bear with me while I try to explain why...

Paranormal investigators are usually very inquisitive, scientifically-minded people, and they usually want to know the reasons *why* a certain type of ghost or haunting occurs. But because we can never be sure of these reasons – certainly not at the time of writing – we tend to turn to our favourite buzzword: theory. When it comes to explaining residual hauntings, there is one particular theory that I, and many others who study paranormal phenomena, turn to. It's called the 'Stone Tape' theory and it goes something like this...

PREVIOUS: *Who knows what you might find lurking around the next corner? One of the display models at* The Falstaff Experience, *Staffordshire, waiting to give unsuspecting investigators a fright!*

Imagine you are walking through your living room and that you are being recorded as you do so, but not by a video camera or any other such device. Imagine the very substances that were used in the construction of your house – the living room walls, for example – were capable of somehow recording you as you pass by and then replaying the images or scene under certain conditions 120 years from that point? Perhaps everything we do is capable of being recorded this way or perhaps it is purely events that are high in emotional content: for example a moment of severe trauma, an overwhelmingly joyous occasion or, rather more macabrely, the split second before death, during which our brain might blast out a huge electrical impulse or impression that is then absorbed and stored by surrounding materials for future broadcast? After all, our brains are seething with powerful electrical impulses.

The 'Stone Tape' theory might go some way to explaining residual hauntings. It could be possible that bricks and stone, for example, are capable of somehow capturing and storing snippets of events that might have happened tens or possibly even hundreds of years previously, and then replaying them like a cinema projection when the correct sort of conditions for playback arise.

This might also go some way to explaining why, when someone experiences these types of ghosts, they report seeing the same scene over and over again, as if the figures or objects involved are stuck in a video replay of the event!

LEFT: *Could it really be possible for the very fabrication of our surroundings to somehow store 'recordings' of past events and replay them like a cinema projection? Some people believe that it could be.*

INTERACTIVE GHOSTS

One thing that is worth remembering if you are ever lucky enough – and yes, I did say lucky enough – to witness this particular type of ghost is not to be too frightened. This type of event is just like watching a repeat on the television, and you are in no danger whatsoever from the ghost you're witnessing!

Interactive ghosts are without a doubt the most widely reported type of ghost – something that is primarily due to the fact that they seem to have numerous ways of making their presence known. They do, however, share one thing in common – they all interact in some way with their surroundings and even with us! It is widely thought that the causes of these phenomena are the spirits of deceased people or animals, who for one reason or another have not yet moved on to a final resting place but remain earthbound and stuck in the realm of the living.

The category that covers interactive ghosts is large and varied, ranging from full-bodied manifestations to smells, and includes the following examples:

1. Full-bodied manifestations

A full-bodied manifestation is by no means the most frequently observed type of ghost, but it is the one that the majority of people associate with the word, as it includes apparitions that walk through walls or disappear before our very eyes. As the term suggests, this type of ghost appears from head to toe in all its glory and often looks just like an ordinary person until it vanishes into thin air, while you scramble for the nearest exit!

2. Partial Manifestations

These are similar to full-bodied manifestations, although I tend to think this type has a rather more frightening appearance. Why? Well imagine the following scenes...

You walk into a room and as you do so you're met with the floating torso of a man! Or, you walk into the room and meet a pair of legs slowly walking towards you, with no torso in sight!

Get the idea? Well I'll tell you one thing – I'd probably be out of that room quicker than a rat wearing running shoes. Don't you think it would be scarier seeing part of a person than the whole thing? I thought so!

3. Voices, Footsteps and Sounds

People often ask me how many ghosts I have seen during my investigations at haunted locations. They are usually somewhat disappointed when I say that I have only ever seen one – and that was the ghost of a cat, which I saw when I lived at my parents' house (see pages 8–11). Perhaps I'm just destined to be one of those people who doesn't get to witness many ghosts, or maybe there's another reason?

Voices, footsteps and sounds are the events that are most frequently experienced and reported within the category that covers interactive ghosts. Of the numerous incidents of ghostly activity recorded, only a relatively small percentage is made up of full- and partial-bodied manifestations. The majority of the remaining events are sounds.

So maybe that's why I haven't seen many ghosts.

You would not believe how many reported incidents describe ghostly sounds. The most common of these are disembodied voices, bangs and thuds, along with the noise that I think outnumbers all others – footsteps. But you can probably think of any sound and you can bet your bottom dollar that some ghost or other has used it to notify us of its presence!

I have heard all of the sounds listed above and on most occasions I could not find any reasonable explanation for their occurrence.

4. Smells

Of the five human senses – sight, hearing, touch, taste and smell – it is the last of these that is the most sensitive. So perhaps it should come as no surprise that unexplained odours, which seem to appear from nowhere, are rather common in the paranormal world, and are quite often associated with ghosts and hauntings. Some of the most widely reported odours include floral scents, particularly roses and lavender, cooking smells and pipe tobacco. Roses and lavender (which is one of the most frequently reported ghostly smells) have long been used in cosmetics: both were often used historically in perfumes. The sudden appearance of one of these distinctive fragrances can often be connected with the presence of a female ghost from a time when these scents predominated. Do such smells evoke an age long gone? Perhaps, but it's worth remembering that while both fragrances were used many years ago, they are also still very popular. And the same applies to just about any other smell!

It is always important to try and find a rational explanation for the source of any unexpected odour at a haunted location – something that is true for the investigation of all paranormal phenomena. And if you can't find a rational explanation, then you may just have struck lucky! And with that little piece of advice, we'll move on to our next type of interactive ghost.

5. Physical Contact

At some point or other there comes a time when every paranormal investigator or individual who hangs around haunted locations often enough experiences physical contact. Now I'm not talking about being punched in the face by the champion prize-fighter of the spirit world here – far from it, although this will become a different matter altogether when we're on the subject of poltergeists (see Chapter 2, pages 20–23). The physical contact I am talking about is much more subtle: for example, hair being gently pulled or stroked, a prodding in your back or the sensation of being touched on your face by invisible fingers. I have had this kind of thing happen to me on a number of occasions, most recently in 2003, when I was gently pushed on my left shoulder. It takes some getting used to, but I can honestly say that – so far – I have not been harmed in any way, shape or form. I have also been lucky enough to witness this type of activity happening to a friend of mine whose hair, which was fairly long and tied back, was lifted and then dropped again!

Maybe this sort of occurrence is evidence of the inquisitive side of ghosts and spirits, or maybe they are simply having some fun with us – who knows? Either way, physical contact with ghosts is nothing to get too alarmed about, so don't worry if it happens to you.

6. Cold Spots

Believe it or not, cold spots are just what the term implies. There's no long-winded scientific explanation for cold spots, but there is, however, a theory attached to them.

A cold spot is a sudden drop in temperature, which usually occurs in a precise area, although they have been known to move about. For example, the whole of a room that you are investigating could be at a constant temperature apart from one small area that is noticeably cooler. Having eliminated all possible causes for this drop in temperature, such as draughty doors and windows, what we are left with is an event termed a 'cold spot' – an area of cold air for which there is no rational explanation.

The theory for cold spots is something like this: every time a ghost tries to do anything, whether it moves an object or manifests itself, it expends energy; eventually, like a battery, its energy resources become depleted and need to be replaced. Imagine if a ghost was capable of drawing that new energy out of the environment it finds itself in, feeding on the heat contained in a room, for example. In the precise area that the ghost absorbed this energy, a cold spot would develop. And if it needed more energy, wouldn't it make sense to move to another location or area where heat (or energy) could be found? This is one explanation for why a cold spot occurs, and could also explain why some are reported to move.

But whatever the cause might be, cold spots are a common occurrence at reputedly haunted locations!

7. Ghostly Mists

This kind of ghost takes the form of a mist-like substance that is often described as being similar to a column of thick, grey fog. There seems to be a number of variations of this type of phenomenon, but the most frequently described is an egg-shaped mist, similar in shape and size to that of a human being. No discernible features are recognizable, and rather than appearing to walk like a human being, the misty form usually seems to float a few inches off the ground, gliding majestically from one place to another.

Nobody really knows why this type of ghost takes on the appearance of a mist – and I must admit that given the option it would not be my preferred choice of ghostly appearance – but it may have something in common with the cold spot theory mentioned above, in that the amount of energy the ghost needs to manifest itself completely isn't readily available.

OPPOSITE: *Stuart Edmonds managed to capture this ghostly mist during an overnight investigation at a haunted priory. Other sources for the mist were ruled out at the time by Stuart.*

ABOVE: *Another unexplained mist, again captured by Stuart Edmonds during an investigation at Staffordshire's Tutbury Castle, where the ghost of Mary Queen of Scots is said to haunt.*

OPPOSITE: *This series of images was captured by Simon Deacon and Steve Griffiths (Swadlincote Paranormal Investigations) during an investigation at a haunted hotel:*
(TOP) *This first image clearly shows a mist developing in the lower right of shot.*
(MIDDLE) *Here the same mist can now been seen over Vince Draper's left shoulder, and it appears to be getting denser, as well as expanding.*
(BOTTOM) *Now the mist has expanded throughout the cellar, is much denser and has taken on a reddish hue.*

The type of ghost that takes on the appearance of a grey mist may also be responsible for another set of widely reported phenomena – the infamous 'Grey Lady' ghosts, which are referred to in an account featured later in the book (see page 97). Now let's move on.

8. Orbs

There are numerous theories and explanations for orbs that examine what they could be and where they come from – believe me, it's a topic that causes much debate!

Just *what* are orbs (or 'globules' as they are also called, particularly in the United States)? At first glance, orbs seem to be moving lights that can appear in various shapes and sizes, although they are predominantly spherical. It is believed by some people that orbs may be the early stages of a ghost or spirit manifestation, and they do actually seem to be prevalent at haunted locations.

The most significant trait of orbs, however, is that they are often only visible under infra-red light: for example, when the 'night-vision' function on a modern digital video camera is in use. They also seem to be captured almost exclusively on digital cameras, which is where the debate begins.

If, as some believe, orbs are actually the first stages of a manifestation, then why is it that we do not seem to be capable of recording any consequent stages or even the full blown article? Surely at a reputedly haunted location where orbs seem to be present, you would think it could only be a matter of time before you succeeded in reaching the 'Holy Grail' of paranormal investigation – a full-bodied manifestation. However, this never seems to be the case. Therefore, could orbs be explained as something closer to the living world than the spirit world?

I have seen a huge amount of orbs during my time as a paranormal investigator, and I have to say that the more I see, the more I am convinced that there is a rational explanation. In my opinion, 99 per cent of orb activity can be explained as dust or other naturally occurring airborne particles. Is it possible that digital video cameras interpret these particles as bright balls of light, which could be some kind of reflection of the infra-red emissions that occur when a digital video camera is in 'night-vision' mode?

A similar thing seems to happen with digital stills cameras too, although these seem to be capable of capturing orbs during the daytime as well as at night. As a photographer friend of mine once pointed out, capturing orbs on these devices could also be a result of the internal workings and components, especially in the way that light sources and their reflections are constructed in the digital environment. For example, if we were to point a normal 35mm camera at a light source and take a photograph, it is more than likely that a set of concentric light reflections (or flares) would be visible on the image when it was developed. But this appears not to be the case where digital stills cameras are concerned. Using a digital camera to take the same shot would result in an entirely different scenario. Digital stills cameras seem not to reveal concentric light reflections, but single and often sporadic points of reflective light that don't necessarily come from the light source. I'm not a professional photographer and I've haven't done any real research on the subject, but check it out and see what results you get.

Whether using a stills camera or video, the word digital seems to be key! However, some paranormal investigators argue that there is a major flaw when citing digital technology as the reason why orbs occur. Why is it that when investigating a haunted location and using a digital video camera in night-vision mode, orb activity occurs when asking for confirmation of spirit presence? And why is it, now that digital stills cameras are used by practically everyone, that the vast majority of orb photographs taken this way appear in supposedly haunted locations? Pure coincidence? I'll let you decide.

2

Poltergeists –
Mind Over Matter

Thanks to the magic of television and film, the subject of this section manages to conjure up all kinds of strange and peculiar monsters that are apparently intent on scaring the wits out of people or dragging their hapless victims into the lowest reaches of Hell. While it might make interesting viewing at the local cinema, I'm afraid to say that the similarities between fictional poltergeists and their paranormal counterparts end there – apart from the scary element!

To begin this section, I think it's important to compare the main differences between what we will call a 'classic' haunting, which involves a ghost, and a haunting, which involves a poltergeist…

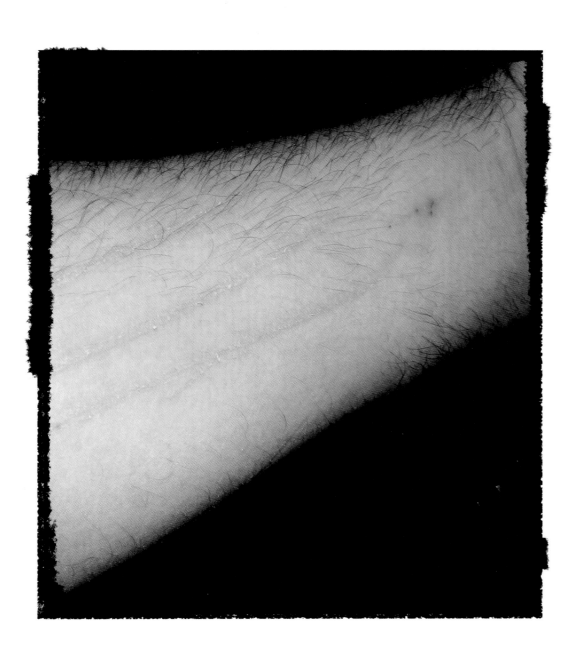

TWO TYPES OF HAUNTING

A classic haunting usually tends to occur in the same place repeatedly, and can last anything from a few months to hundreds of years. As described earlier (see pages 15–16), the type of phenomena associated with a haunting of this kind is usually sensory – hearing noises, smelling odours, feeling cold spots and possibly gentle physical contact – with the bulk of these experiences fairly low in intensity.

Occasionally a sighting of some description may be witnessed and objects may move.

'Poltergeist' comes from the German for 'noisy spirit'. They are not ghosts in the true meaning of the word and a haunting of this type rarely lasts longer than a few months (in some cases only weeks). The phenomena associated with this type of haunting are very physical in nature: furniture or other objects might be moved, stones may be thrown (a very common occurrence) and, in some rare instances, actual physical harm may come to the individual or individuals unlucky enough to be in the locality.

Other activities that come under the umbrella of a poltergeist haunting include both the sudden appearance and/or disappearance of objects – an event called an *apport*; pleasant or foul smells; strange writings; interference with electrical appliances and strange, discarnate voices. Occasionally a sighting of one type or another is witnessed – something this type of event has in common with a 'classic' kind of haunting. In summary, a poltergeist haunting is much more physical than a classic haunting and much more intense.

Looking For an Explanation

As I have stated before, it's always important to look for any rational causes of a suspected paranormal incident. In the case of poltergeist activity, there are several possible questions to be considered:

1. Could vibrations have caused an object to move unexpectedly? For example, is the location where the movement occurred close to any heavily-used main roads? Are there any railway lines or underground train lines nearby that could cause vibration? Were there any minor earth tremors recorded – and these do occur much more regularly than we may think – on the day that the object seemed to move? Even the very smallest of tremors can produce surprisingly powerful, but subliminal, vibrations.

2. If strange noises were heard, can they be easily explained? For example, a gust of wind blowing down a chimney can create all sorts of unusual noises, and can cause windows to rattle unexpectedly and doors to slam shut. Wind can blow things over too, causing yet more startling noises.

3. Were there any thunderstorms in the vicinity when you experienced strange electrical interference? It is also worth bearing in mind that a storm does not necessarily have to be directly overhead to have an adverse affect on electrical systems or appliances. Where cases involving the interference of electrical systems and appliances are

PREVIOUS: *One of the most frequently reported occurrences during particularly aggressive poltergeist cases are scratches. Other activity includes throwing objects, noises and foul smells.*

LEFT: *Poltergeist activity is very physical in nature, ranging from small objects being moved around to actual harm coming to individuals unfortunate enough to be in the vicinity.*

concerned, it's a well-known fact that lightning and thunderstorms can cause all manner of problems, including flickering lights; light bulbs blowing; interference on telephone lines and, in severe cases, televisions and radios blowing up. It's also worth checking to see if there was there any kind of local power failure that could have been responsible for the interference.

All of these points should be carefully considered before concluding whether or not the activities witnessed were the work of a poltergeist. In any case, one thing is for certain: there's no big budget monster appearing from an out-of-this-world portal to swallow up your house and surrounding neighbourhood!

Poltergeist Theory

I suppose this section wouldn't be complete without a theory or two about the poltergeist phenomenon.

The first theory is that poltergeist activity is caused by spirits that are unhappy because we are occupying the same space as them. To indicate their discontent, they disrupt our lives in one or more of the ways described above, attempting to drive us away and leave them in peace. This, as you would imagine, often achieves the desired result. After all, who in their right mind would want to remain in a situation like that for longer than is necessary? Those who do find themselves staying put usually find other ways and means of trying to dispel their unwelcome guest and sometimes, as a last resort, end up contacting a person of religious standing with a view to blessing the property in which these unwanted activities are occurring. I must add, though, that this kind of procedure does seem to have a hit and miss outcome and the poltergeist activity usually returns over time.

The second theory is utterly different, but is certainly one that I rather like the sound of. In a lot of poltergeist cases there seems to be a specific person, known as a 'focus', who is at the centre of the activity. More often than not this focus is a young male or female experiencing a stressful period in their lives, such as puberty.

The thinking surrounding this theory revolves around how the brain reacts under heightened emotional conditions. It considers the role the brain might have when it comes to understanding poltergeists and their associated activities. For example, what if severe stress or

huge emotional tension over a long period of time causes the brain to produce 'Subconscious Psychokinetic Energies' (SPE), during which the very power of the brain causes the sorts of events that are often attributed to the activities of a poltergeist?

As we all know the brain is extremely powerful and forms the control centre for everything that we do. Despite huge advances in technology and medicine, there are still areas of the brain whose functionality and capability have not been fully explained. Is it possible that these hitherto unknown areas of the brain are responsible for strange actions under the correct mental conditions? For example, when frustration builds it is often revealed in a sudden outburst of anger. This could also be what happens in cases of poltergeist activity, in that a person under immense emotional pressure projects enough psychokinetic energy out of the brain to move furniture, throw objects and even harm people through severe, subconscious mental frustration.

A Famous Poltergeist

There have been many noted cases of poltergeist activity, but arguably the most famous – or infamous – of all involved a family from the Enfield area in North London.

The 'Enfield Poltergeist', as it was known, terrorized the family during the 1970s and was responsible for all manner of frightening occurrences, including strange voices, items violently thrown and objects and furniture moved. On one occasion two young female members of the family were apparently dragged out of bed and thrown through the air!

Paranormal expert and investigator Maurice Grosse placed the house under surveillance and documented numerous unexplained incidents. He was soon joined by a press photographer, which resulted in some of the most talked about and controversial images ever witnessed, including pictures of the two girls in mid-flight, having been thrown from their beds!

It is a fascinating case and was well documented. The various occurences highlighted some of the more extreme poltergeist phenomena and reports of the case are certainly worth reading – should you be brave enough. However, as with any paranormal case you read about, please make up your own minds and come to your own conclusions about the events recounted.

3

'N' is for 'Nasty'

D on't panic! The chances are that you will never encounter one of the entities that I'm about to describe, but, as the saying goes, if you play on the motorway long enough you will eventually get hit by a car.

Before going any further I can honestly say that I have yet to encounter an unpleasant entity and have never actually been physically harmed during my years of paranormal investigating.

There are numerous names for 'nasty entities', although they are sometimes labelled 'dark', 'demonic' or 'negative'. They usually occur when some kind of summoning device is utilized, particularly if it is being used by individuals who do not know what they are doing or precisely what they could be dealing with.

OUIJA BOARDS AND DARK ARTS

The most common summoning device by far is the ouija board. The word 'ouija' is a combination of the French and German words for 'yes' – 'oui' and 'ja'. The apparatus consists of a board with numbers, letters and words printed on its surface and a device called a 'planchette', which is typically made from wood and more often than not is triangular in shape. It can also have a pencil affixed to it. Glasses are also sometimes used.

The individual or individuals taking part – known as 'sitters' – rest their fingers lightly on the planchette, which is positioned on the board. Those involved then ask for any spirit present to communicate with them.

The sitters usually ask the spirit or spirits questions. In reply, the spirit or spirits move the planchette, spelling out the answers using the letters and symbols on the board. The inherent problem with this type of spirit communication is that it is very difficult to control what you are dealing with – and even more difficult to find out whether you're dealing with a good or bad guy, so to speak.

Many incidents that have recorded troublesome or demonic entities encountered via an ouija board or other summoning device describe how the spirit communicating with the sitters initially seems sincere and genuine and readily answers any questions asked. As the questioning continues, the sitters often begin to trust what the spirit is saying or the spirit's apparent identity. It is at this point that serious problems begin to occur.

Some of these problems are physical in nature and similar to those encountered in cases of poltergeist activity (see Chapter 2, pages 20–23), although the two types of event are not considered to be directly connected. Sometimes the entity communicating with the sitters starts to lie when answering questions, a scenario that can prove to be very upsetting for those involved. There have even been incidents that have caused families and friends to have huge arguments after believing what they have heard or been told via an ouija board.

Another problem is that once an entity has been summoned in this fashion it is often very difficult to get rid of it. Therefore, I would not advise the use of ouija boards and summoning devices.

Other forms of negative or demonic entity arise from different means altogether, often as the result of people dabbling with what are termed the 'black arts' and other extreme occult practices.

If we are to believe certain reports it would seem that many 'nasty' entities exist that can cause physical damage and even mental harm in extreme cases, although most investigators would agree that this is quite a rare occurrence. Usually the only way to be rid of a 'dark' entity is to have some kind of blessing or cleansing ritual performed, normally by a person of religious standing. However, as stated earlier, this can sometimes make things worse and the ritual may need repeating several times if the case is extreme. The following incident concerning a ouija board was related to me many moons ago by one of the sitters – my mother! Although there were no longstanding ill-effects from this particular encounter, it did leave a lasting impression on all of those who took part. In fact, it made such an impression on my mother that she never took part in anything like it again, and often warned me against messing about with things beyond the physical world. Here is my mother's story for you to read, digest and come to your own conclusions about.

The Ouija Board Incident

My mother Ann is the second of three children, her siblings being her younger brother, Richard, and older sister Cynthia. In 1961, when my mother was about 12 years old, the three of them decided to have a go at making an ouija board, as their mother had been scaring them with talk of ghosts and spirits.

The Grand National horse race, which takes place every year at Aintree, Liverpool, was fast approaching, and the three children could think of no better question to ask the board than for the winner of this prestigious event, presumably thinking of the sweets and other goodies they would buy with their winnings.

And so, they wrote the alphabet on a piece of cardboard took an upturned glass and proceeded to conjure up a them with an answer.

None of them thought that anything would happen – after all what spirit would want to talk to a bunch of children? But they still thought they would give it a go – the prospect of easy pocket money was just irresistible. So they sat around an old, blue formica table in the kitchen and started to ask for any spirit or ghost present to come and talk to them with the now familiar question, 'Is there anybody there?' A few seconds passed and the glass began to move, making its way towards the word 'YES', which was written on the board.

This astonished the three children, but secretly each was blaming one of the others for the moving glass. With the glass now firmly positioned on 'YES', Richard proceeded to invite the others to ask for the winner of the Grand National, although he didn't really expect any kind of response to be forthcoming.

After pondering things for a few moments, perhaps in an air of uncertainty, the other two agreed and politely requested whatever spirit may be with them (if any) to give them the information they needed. They sat patiently, each with their middle finger on the overturned glass, waiting for some kind of movement. Nothing.

Thinking somehow that if they asked in a louder voice they would get a better reaction, they repeated the question. Almost immediately the glass started moving and made towards the letter 'N'. With each of them still believing that one of the other two was providing the momentum for the glass moving, they kept their fingers gently touching the glass, which was now changing course and heading towards the letter 'I'.

This trend continued, landing on 'C', 'H', 'O', 'L', 'A' and 'S' respectively. Each of the three insisted that they were

ABOVE: *Séances and other attempts at communicating with the spirit world were commonplace during the Victorian era.*

not moving the glass, and all three started to panic simultaneously while the glass carried on its journey across the board, eventually ending on the 'R' of 'SILVER'.

Totally freaked out and rather upset, the three children quickly gathered up the board, ripped it into pieces, smashed the glass, depositing everything in the dustbin.

As you may be aware, the board spelled out the words 'NICHOLAS SILVER'. A few days after the ouija board session a runner that was only the second grey horse to ever win the Grand National came home ahead of the field to claim the first prize. Its name was Nicholas Silver. The year was 1961. From that day onwards, my mother, her sister and brother never attempted contact with the spirit world again.

This is a fascinating story made even more interesting by the fact that it is perfectly true. Whatever the source of the moving glass, spiritual or otherwise, it was enough to alter the minds and thoughts of three children and have an effect on them in adulthood too.

4

Some More Theories

One thing that has always puzzled me about ghosts is the remarkable knack that they have of vanishing just as the witness does a 'double take' – they might look away momentarily, perhaps to reflect on what they have seen, but when they look back the ghost has disappeared. Is this something that ghosts and spirits constantly practise or take lessons in? Is there some sort of 'Ghost Behaviour School' that teaches a would-be ghost the required etiquette before they are given their haunting licence? I highly doubt it, although you never know! There could, of course, be a more realistic explanation for the above scenario – the workings of the human brain!

In those moments when the mind enters a state of relaxation, even subconsciously, and leaves behind the worries and concerns of everyday life, are we more susceptible to witnessing the ghosts or spirits of the deceased? Let me try and explain...

GHOSTS OF THE MIND?

The mind, as you would imagine, is a very complex piece of equipment that is common to every human being. Even with the advanced level of scientific knowledge we have these days, nobody is really able to say exactly how it works or what it is capable of achieving – anything could be possible really.

So what if, once completely relaxed, we are capable of tuning into different frequencies or invisible dimensions that exist, as some have speculated, alongside our own, and that we cannot normally see – frequencies or dimensions in which ghosts or spirit entities exist? It could be possible.

Remember, just because we can't see something, it doesn't mean it doesn't exist. We can't ordinarily see the air we breathe in and out, but it's there! Picture the scene I'm about to describe...

You are walking through a supposedly haunted location, for example, the Tower of London. As you stroll through the historic fort, you begin to lose yourself in the magnificent sights that this grand building has to offer with its long and fascinating history. You have forgotten for the moment all your usual concerns, the worries and stresses that a typical person encounters on a daily basis, such as work, money, bills and the like.

At this point, you see something totally out of character with the modern world – a woman dressed in spectacular 16th-century clothing walking towards you.

For no more than a split second you avert your gaze, to clear your head or perhaps to ponder what you have seen, but when you return your eyes to the spot at which you were looking just a moment ago, you discover the figure has disappeared.

How and why would something that you would swear you had seen so clearly, simply vanish in the split second or so that you looked away from it? Surely that brief amount of time shouldn't make much difference – or should it?

PREVIOUS: *The paranormal world is full of unanswered questions: what, why, where and how?*

Well, look at it this way. When you first glimpsed the woman, your mind was in a state of relaxation and had perhaps tuned into a certain specific frequency or dimension that allowed you to see the ghost. However, in the split second or so that you looked away from the woman and attempted to make sense of what you had just seen, your mind automatically clicked back into its normal 'rational' state. Such is the huge complexity of the brain, that even over the course of that short period of time it would have been working like crazy, and going through immeasurable thought processes and calculations. In that split second, the essential state of mind needed to see a ghost or spirit is lost.

Could this go some way to explaining why several people in a group often claim to see the same ghost at the same time? Is it because the witnesses are all mentally relaxed and therefore tuned into the required viewing frequency or dimension?

Magnetic Persuasion
Magnetic fields are a topic of continued debate as far as paranormal experiences are concerned. Why?

Well, there are some individuals out there who would like to place the blame for incidents involving paranormal activity on the presence of magnetic fields. Not only are we constantly subjected to the various naturally-occurring magnetic fields that surround our planet, but we also routinely experience certain forms of man-made electro-magnetic radiation that is constantly being emitted from objects ranging from domestic appliances to overhead power-lines and electricity sub-stations.

There are those people who believe that magnetic fields are powerful enough and affect the brain to such an extent that they cause people close enough to the source of such emissions to imagine anomalous phenomena or imagine strange episodes.

Scientists have actually studied the possible effects of electromagnetic radiation on the brain, by carrying out a varied range of experiments on volunteers in controlled conditions. The subject of a test like this would be fitted with a helmet that is full of all manner of equipment designed to bombard the brain with magnetic impulses.

The individual who is being studied may be placed in differing states of sensory deprivation. For example, the subject's eyes might be covered over; the subject might be fitted with headphones that are playing 'white noise', which sounds similar to radio static; they may also be shut in a darkened room with nothing but a red light shining onto them.

Under conditions like these, the individuals under scrutiny have reported all kinds of sensations, some of which could certainly be mistaken for paranormal phenomena of one kind or another. For example, volunteers often feel that there is someone else in the room with them and that they are being watched; they may also feel as if they are being touched or experience inexplicable feelings of fear. Freaky or what! And pretty convincing evidence, don't you think?

Well, this is all well and good, but many other people would argue in reponse that the strength of the magnetic field that would be required for these kinds of effect to happen outside of laboratory conditions has yet to be proved. Even those in the world of parapsychology argue this point and that's a turn up for the books! But what about other naturally occurring conditions, for example geographical fault lines?

Fault lines are basically cracks that occur within the Earth's crust – a very famous example of this being the San Andreas Fault, which is located in the USA. These geological wonders are found all over our planet, and range from tiny cracks to huge gashes in the land that can run more miles along their length. Fault lines are usually prone to a seismic activity. This term covers a wide range of phenomena – not always on the destructive scale we associate with massive earthquakes! Seismic waves in actual fact can produce certain types of tremor that are almost subliminal, as I talked about earlier in the book (see page 22).

Seismic tremors can cause objects to move, items to fall off shelves, things to fall over and even make you believe that some kind of paranormal activity is taking place if you are caught off guard.

I experienced this very effect first hand a few years ago. It was about 2 o'clock in the morning and I was sound asleep, when all of a sudden I became aware that my bed was vibrating, as if somebody was shaking it gently. I also became aware of a noise, which sounded as if my washing machine was in its spin cycle. I even ventured downstairs to see if I had left it on by accident, but it was switched off.

This experience had only lasted for a period of about seven seconds or so, although it seemed longer at the time mainly because I had been roused from my deep state of slumber. Anyway, I was very confused and more than slightly concerned that I had been woken by some wandering poltergeist intent on making my home its new place of residence when sleep took over. I should add that my home had already been subject to some strange episodes, which I explain in detail earlier in the book (see pages 8–11).

The following morning, over breakfast, I began to give my parents a detailed account of what had happened in the early hours of the morning. They both started to laugh and proceeded to tell me that an earth tremor had taken place in the small hours of the morning some 50 miles away! My parents and many others had experienced my supposed 'poltergeist activity'!

It's important to remember at this point that, although my own experience in this case was quite noticeable, most of the time we don't even realize tremors are occurring – unless of course there's a seismograph set up in your spare room!

I think it is also worth mentioning that there do seem to be quite a few apparently haunted locations situated on or near known fault lines. Is this the cause of the paranormal activity and hauntings that occur at these locations? Well perhaps, and it could certainly account for the strange movement of objects, don't you think? But what about the fact that people *see* things at these locations. How can an earth tremor cause this to happen?

When fault lines cause a tremor, even those we may not necessarily feel on a physical level, an incredible release of electromagnetic energy will often occur. Could this release of energy perhaps affect the brain to such a degree that it momentarily causes a hallucinatory experience, causing individuals to think that they are seeing a ghost or spirit? Well, it might explain why visual experiences of ghosts are so sporadic.

However, don't forget that – as I mentioned towards the beginning of this section, there is no real proof outside of controlled laboratory conditions that magnetic or electro-magnetic energy causes these experiences.

5

Investigation Equipment

As with every investigation the main objectives are to try and capture some kind of proof for the existence of paranormal phenomena, while learning as much as we can along the way. The right equipment can make a big difference to your investigations!

Please bear in mind, however, when using certain gadgets, such as an EMF meter or a motion detector unit, that while such devices may aid a paranormal investigation, their use has not been scientifically proven for such tasks. As such, any evidence gathered through the use of these devices should be examined thoroughly.

EQUIPMENT

In today's gadget-filled world, paranormal investigators can call upon a number of devices that will aid this type of quest; what follows is a list some of the items that are useful, complete with handy guidelines on how to use each of them:

A. PAPER AND PENCILS

Although paper and pencils are not new to the world of paranormal investigation, they are always useful to have on hand, and allow you to write reports, make detailed observations or even draw sketches that record the movement or trajectory of objects observed.

Always try to get into the habit of noting down the time at which you think that any possible paranormal activity might have occurred, as it makes record-keeping an awful lot easier and helps to get rid of the 'Umm, err' factor, for example:

'What time was it when we saw that full-bodied manifestation?'

'Umm, err... I'm not sure!'

Tip: This may sound trivial, but make sure you also carry a pencil sharpener with you.

B. THERMOMETER

Thermometers are always beneficial during a paranormal investigation, and I would advise using a modern digital device if at all possible. Nowadays these are relatively inexpensive and very accurate. They can also reveal temperature fluctuations much more quickly than standard thermometers. Some digital thermometers also have a function that allows the user to recall the minimum and maximum temperatures recorded, which proves extremely useful when trying to establish cold spots. It is always handy to have several thermometers set up at the location under investigation and to check them periodically, noting any unusual fluctuations.

Tip: It's common sense, but make sure you place any thermometers in a draught-free area.

C. DICTAPHONES AND TAPE RECORDERS

Dictaphones are great little devices and these days they are available in two formats – analogue or digital. The analogue variety uses a particular type of cassette tape on which sounds are recorded (called a mini-cassette). A digital dictaphone on the other hand does not have any type of cassette. Instead it uses digital technology to record and store sound. The digital files can be saved and transferred to a computer.

Both of these types of device have their advantages and disadvantages. An analogue dictaphone is cheap and the mini-cassettes are easily replaced when they run out; however, these devices cannot be connected to a computer. A digital dictaphone is smaller than its analogue counterpart and most models can be easily connected to a computer; however, they are fairly expensive and, once they are full of audio data you have to either erase some of the material or download it to a computer before you can use the device again.

Most dictaphones, whether analogue or digital, usually contain a feature that allows recording to be activated without the user present. The device is simply set up as desired and switches to record mode when triggered by an audible sound.

I have used both types of dictaphone, and must admit that I do prefer the digital models over analogue devices, as they allow greater analysis and manipulation of recordings using a computer and the accompanying editing software.

Tape recorders are also available in digital and analogue formats. These devices are also extremely useful when conducting paranormal investigations.

Tip: If using analogue recording gear, make sure you have spare batteries with you as well as tape. Also, try walking around a location while holding a recording device and asking questions to a spirit, checking the recorded results later.

D. MOTION DETECTORS

Motion detectors are devices that – would you believe it – detect movement! They are relatively cheap to buy and provide an invaluable tool during paranormal investigations. The motion detectors available today usually operate using infra-red technology. Basically, the device emits an invisible beam of infra-red light and

anything that breaks this beam triggers an alarm of some kind, alerting members of the investigating team.

For example, if a ghost has been observed walking from one room to another, then the motion detector should be positioned in the correct place to intersect its path. Therefore, theoretically at least, if the ghost puts in another appearance, it will cross the beam, break it and trigger the alarm.

As with most of the devices that are listed here, it is always advantageous to have more than one motion detector on site during an investigation.

Tip: *Always* make sure your fellow team members know where motion detectors are set up. Not only is it annoying to have to keep resetting them, but it can be very alarming to set one off by mistake if you didn't know it was there!

E. VIDEO CAMERA

Video cameras are becoming more and more affordable and they are increasingly popular for use on paranormal investigations. What's more, you don't need to be a famous Hollywood film director with a penchant for homesick aliens to use one!

Video cameras serve a two-fold purpose: with luck they record any paranormal activity that might occur during an investigation and they also safeguard against interference from human sources.

These days, more often than not, video cameras are digital and they are usually equipped with a night-vision

function that uses infra-red technology to allow you to record in total darkness. This function is especially handy, as most paranormal investigations seem to take place in darkened conditions or during the night. As discussed earlier in this book, digital cameras seem to be particularly adept at capturing paranormal phenomena known as orbs (see pages 18–19). It is certainly worth bearing some of the points raised in that section in mind when reviewing footage shot with a digital video camera using night-vision mode.

Tip: When using the night-vision function, try not to point cameras towards one another, as the infra-red beams will clash, resulting in very bad 'white-glare'. The same thing also happens when reflections of the beam are picked up in a mirror or a window.

F. ELECTROMAGNETIC FIELD (EMF) METER

An Electromagnetic Field (EMF) meter is a useful piece of kit for paranormal investigations, but, as with all electronic devices, it does require you to read the operating instructions carefully prior to use. The EMF meters that most paranormal investigators use cost between £45–200 (US$75–350). These devices detect subtle changes in electromagnetic fields, which some people believe could indicate the presence of paranormal phenomena or recent paranormal activity.

One theory about ghosts suggests that they emit a slightly stronger magnetic field whenever they try to manifest or cause some form of paranormal activity, or that they somehow interfere with naturally occurring magnetic fields, which causes a slight rise in readings. Whatever the particular reason, if any kind of electromagnetic fluctuation is detected during an investigation, it can be measured on an EMF meter. The strength of the electromagnetic fluctuation is measured in milligauss, or mG for short, and indicated on the display that is incorporated into such devices.

Most paranormal investigators will tell you that a measurement reading of 2–8mG could be indicative of paranormal activity or a ghostly presence. However, this might not be the case, as we are surrounded by different pieces of equipment that also emit electromagnetic waves, such as televisions, radios, computers, lighting and power cables – the list is endless. This is why it is important to conduct a series of baseline readings before your investigation begins (see pages 46–47).

Tip: Try not to make erratic movements when using an EMF meter, as some models, especially those with an audible sensor or detection signal, have been known to give a false reading. Keep your movements slow and smooth.

G. TRIGGER OBJECTS

Trigger objects are small items that are used with the sole purpose of getting some kind of interaction from whatever might be haunting the location that is under investigation. Some of the most common trigger objects used are things such as marbles, coins, small bells or wooden crosses. Experiments using trigger objects are explained in more depth later on (see pages 48–50).

Tip: As well as using your imagination when selecting trigger objects, you may want to try using something that has a connection with whatever is thought to be haunting the location you are investigating. For instance, if the ghost is thought to be that of a child then use a small toy or a sweet.

H. FLOUR OR TALCUM POWDER

These two items come in very useful when using certain trigger objects, but they can also be used for dusting surfaces like wooden floors or tabletops. For instance, if there is a room where footsteps have frequently been heard, then try dusting an area of the floor and sealing off the room. If anything walks on the dusted surface it will leave imprints, which could give clues as to what is causing the haunting.

Tip: Again, it's common sense, but do not use flour or talcum powder on damp surfaces!

I. TORCHES

A torch is an invaluable piece of equipment for every paranormal investigation and each member of your team should have one – especially if you are conducting your research at night. Also make sure that you carry several sets of replacement batteries – it is not uncommon for batteries to drain mysteriously in haunted locations, and if they do run out you're in for a night of severe eye-strain. Of course, you could always try munching on a carrot or two should you forget them!

Tip: You can buy battery-free torches, which you wind up – if you can be bothered to crank them up every few minutes!

J. WALKIE-TALKIES

These are an absolute necessity for all investigations, especially those that involve a large group of individuals that is dispersed throughout the location. Walkie-talkies are relatively cheap to purchase.

Tip: Make sure your walkie-talkies are charged before an investigation and that you have enough to go round if your team splits into smaller groups.

K. CANDLES

A word of warning here – you must always be *very* careful when using candles and *always* observe fire safety rules... The absolute last thing you want is an unexpected bonfire on your hands.

Candles are very useful not only as a secondary light source but also for helping to identify where a particular draught is coming from, thus helping to eliminate any false cold spots that might be encountered. They are also good for checking around the edges of windows and doors for any external breezes that might be mistaken as being paranormal in origin.

A candle's flame will always flicker in the opposite direction to that of the draught, i.e. if a draught is coming from the left of the candle flame, it will flicker to the right and vice versa.

Tip: Never leave candles unattended.

6

Mediums and Psychics

M any paranormal investigation groups have a medium who accompanies them on their investigations, in order to give the team their 'impressions' (as they are often called) of what or who might be haunting a certain location and why. It can be quite astonishing to have a medium, who does not know anything about the location they are investigating, giving out rarely known information that is found to be correct upon post investigation research.

As I am not an expert in mediumship or psychics I have asked my good friend, renowned medium Dave Wharmby of the Bassetlaw Ghost Research Group, to give us an insight into mediumship and what it involves.

Dave has kindly compiled this next section, for which I sincerely thank him…

THE TYPES OF MEDIUM

I have been very lucky in my career, as I have worked alongside some of the most famous mediums in the business. Mediums, or psychics as they are sometimes known, are individuals who appear, for the most part, to have a special 'gift' – they can 'see', 'hear' or 'feel' things beyond what are recognized as normal, human functions. Some even claim to be able to communicate with the spirits of the deceased. There are several forms of medium ability:

Clairaudient mediums – These individuals have the ability to hear things outside what is recognized as normal human perception.

Clairsentient mediums – These individuals are able to sense, feel and recognize events before they have taken place.

Clairvoyant mediums – These individuals can see things beyond what is deemed 'normal' human vision.

Some mediums have just one of these abilities; others have all of them. One thing that nearly all mediums and psychics have in common is that they communicate through a named 'spirit guide'. This is a spirit who guides, advises, protects and informs the medium with all manner of information in relation to their work. For instance, my good friend and former work colleague, the world-renowned spirit-medium Derek Acorah, has a spirit guide called 'Sam' who helps him in gathering his information in relation to his work as a psychic and medium.

Anyway, without further ado, let me hand you over to renowned medium Dave Wharmby of the Bassetlaw Ghost Research Group. I have worked with Dave and his lovely wife Fran on numerous occasions and have to admit that they are two of the most down-to-earth people you could meet.

I hope this little section will help to shed a clearer light on the world of mediumship. Although this section cannot hope to be exhaustive, I hope it provides you with some food for thought.

PREVIOUS: *The mysterious 'crystal ball'. Although these devices are used, the majority of mediums and psychics use no such objects when gathering their information.*

LEFT: *During attempts to contact ghosts or spirits, some investigators are aided by particular items, such as dowsing rods, crystals or, as in this picture, the pendulum. The pendulum either swings back and forth, side to side, or in a circular motion, in answer to questions posed.*

DAVE WHARMBY – PSYCHIC MEDIUM

Many of you reading this book may already have a little insight into what a medium is. However, is a medium merely someone that gives us messages from the departed [spirit], messages of comfort and advice... or is there more to it than this?

There are many forms of mediumship and they can be given many different titles: from 'psychic' to 'clairvoyant' to 'medium'. But there are also 'trance mediums', 'transfiguration mediums' and 'physical mediums'. So firstly, let's look at the various types of medium and what these actually are.

All of the above involve a person who has in some way developed their ability to connect to the other side [the spirit world], and this could be any one of you right now who is reading this very book, for we are all born with the ability of connecting in different ways to spirits, but of course it is your own choice as to whether you follow it through or merely ignore it.

There is not a lot of difference between an individual with psychic and clairvoyant abilities, for both of them have clairaudience, clairsentience, or clairvoyance (see opposite for definitions of these). Of these, clairsentience is the basic form of the ability most of us possess.

'Medium' is merely the term given to a person who has progressed to different levels of spirit communication. Incidentally, spirits can and do work with many people in many forms. Some people, like myself, work directly with spirits, while others work through the use of Tarot cards, crystals, rune stones, psychic art etc... the list goes on.

Anyway, let us now examine the different types or levels of mediumship.

More often than not, the medium works in a manner that provides personal messages and an insight into a person's future events, working alongside individuals who have come forward from the spirit world to act as helpers or guides in their life.

A trance medium works in a manner that allows spirits to 'channel' through them; in other words they allow a

spirit presence to enter into their body and speak directly to those people who are present, often in their own voice.

A transfiguration medium is also like a trance medium, but instead allows spirits to work even closer with them – often to the point at which a spirit presence can be seen to alter the appearance of the medium visually so you can actually see the face of that spirit person as they speak through the medium.

Lastly, there is also the category of physical mediumship. This is where the medium allows a spirit presence to use either direct energy or ectoplasm [a strange substance that is believed to emanate from a medium during some forms of spirit communication, often white in colouration] to create a wonderful phenomenon to those witnessing the occasion.

During a trance-like state, a physical medium can create a form of energy whereby spirits can and often do actually appear as a solid form in the same room as them; they speak directly to those present and can even touch them physically – just as a solid, live person would.

So how do all of these processes actually work?

As stated previously, we are all born with a psychic ability, and this is most prominently seen in small children for, as I am sure you will agree, young children are innocent in mind, innocent of the world and all of its misgivings and badness, are totally open-minded, and as a result ideal to see and witness spirit presences.

This is probably why there are so many widespread reports of children having what are often dismissed as 'imaginary friends'... However, are they so imaginary? Maybe when your child is apparently chattering away to themselves you ought to listen more closely to the kind of conversation they are having, as you might be surprised to find that it is on an intelligent level and not just nonsense...

So these are the different levels of mediumship, but how does a medium actually feel (or, come to that, any person) when a spirit presence is around?

I can only speak from my own personal, experiences and from those of others who have told me what they feel, but the process often affects different people in different ways. The sensing of a spirit presence can be as simple as a smell: that is, you may have come across a smell that is associated with one of your loved ones, be it from a certain tobacco or pipe smell, to an aftershave, perfume or even something related to a past person's employment – for example, cleaning fluids or polish. These smells are often brought to us to help us recognise who this might be or what they did: this is a form of clairsentience.

I have personally experienced the above as well as all of the following: a headache, dry lips, a tight chest, nausea and even a sense of swaying, all when a spirit-being is present.

But how do I and other mediums actually connect or communicate with a spirit presence?

This can be done in one or more ways, but the most common of all is thought transference, whereby the spirit speaks to the medium by placing the thoughts or words in their mind and allowing the medium to understand what is being said, or by voices in the ear [clairaudience].

When a spirit presence communicates with me, I will experience both of these; on occasion, I and those around me at the time, have also experienced a form of heat – a glowing sensation – that seems to emanate from me, normally when I'm about to go into a trance-like state.

Trance is like a form of deep meditation or self-hypnosis that allows the medium to be totally open-minded in order to receive a spirit presence within their body and make direct communication. All of this must seem very complicated to many, but I would really emphasise that it is second or even first nature to the vast majority of us, and it is within everyone's capability to be a medium in some manner or other.

My first direct experience of a spirit presence was at the age of nine, when I literally heard many spirits calling out to me [clairaudience]. Of course at that time I was too young to understand what this actually was and what it meant. My parents, however, being very religious and devout Christians, felt that some form of demonic presence was trying to attack me when I spoke to them about it; so it was a case of down on the floor and praying to God as a family for protection. Now of course I laugh at this very concept, as I have come to know and understand the spirit world.

It wasn't until I reached the age of 18 that I next encountered a spirit presence.

After my first experience, which had left a lasting effect upon me (not as in fear but more curiosity), I knew that I needed to search more. After leaving the confines of my religious home at 16 and stepping out into the big bad world, I began my quest. I examined numerous religious movements and even joined a couple, mainly to see where they were coming from. It was during my time with the Unification Church (better known to many as the Moonies), that a spirit presence came to me once more.

One night while I was asleep and in a dream state, a clear and vivid message told me I was seeking the truth in the wrong place and that I needed to look more within myself to find the answers. This in itself was strange enough, but what followed next was stranger still.

One of my fads of the day was to rise at 5.30 am and jog for an hour and I always took the same route through the local park. A couple of days after I had had my dream and while I was out on my morning jog I saw a spirit. It appeared to me as a moving black shape – like a man draped in the garment of a monk. However, as I witnessed this apparition, I realised that it was not running in front of me or even walking, but actually gliding across the footpath and then it disappeared into the neighbouring woods. Well my jog turned into a sprint that day, but after the initial shock, my mind once more kicked into rationalisation and I began questioning what I had actually seen.

It appeared that the pathway through which I jogged every morning had been a pilgrim's route back in the Middle Ages and many a visiting monk had used it on their way to a local monastery. So had I seen a monk? I was later to discover that, in actual fact, I had.

My interest in ghosts became fired and I mixed with various other inquisitive minds – even students from a section of Bristol College, who were examining the paranormal phenomena, although most of them were 'rookies' and many were trying to find an obvious form of explanation through science.

It is funny to look back and see how life takes us all off on different journeys: I had been given a great taster of things to come, almost preparing me for what lay ahead in my life. It wasn't until several years later that the spirit world then decided that it was the right time for me to wake up and get started.

I used to have a regular babysitter and one day we were talking about ghosts, when I suddenly began to feel very shaky and developed a headache. I then started to quiz her about her family, or rather actually tell her about family members who had passed away. I don't know who was the most shocked – me or her!

I even started to hear her grandfather speak to me, who said something which I knew I could not repeat. After the babysitter had gone home I told my friends that her grandfather had spoken of her grandmother and that he was waiting to take her into spirit the same day. They told me that I was mad, but sure enough, a few days later we heard that our sitter's grandmother had indeed passed away the day after her visit! Now I knew something was afoot, but still failed to act further upon it until a tragedy in my life shook me.

Without going into all the details, I had a daughter who passed away at the age of two and half (a total of six years ago now). Before this, certain dreams would come and I would always try to ignore them. But, on the day my daughter died, the spirit world made its presence abundantly clear. Firstly, my eldest daughter began seeing her own late grandmother every night for about a week before her sister died. True, I did sense something or someone in her room, but felt that perhaps she was over-reacting until the actual day.

Furthermore, a bizarre set of events happened, which could not have been of a natural source, leading up to her passing.

On the day of her funeral I carried the coffin to the grave myself, but through distress I felt I was losing my grip, until I felt a small pair of hands grasping around my own and a voice clearly saying, 'It's okay, Dad, I will help you.' Suddenly a surge of strength filled me and enabled me to continue what I was doing.

A few weeks passed and a need arose in me to contact a medium to find out if my daughter was all right: clearly then and unknowingly I had come to believe and accept that the spirit world existed. At the time I was reading a book written by a certain medium whose name eludes me. I felt she was the one I needed to speak with. I had no address, only a name and an area, but surprise, surprise, she was the only one listed for that area in the phone book. I rang her and was told she was booked solid for at least the next 10 months. Disheartened, I decided to leave it for a while, but the very next day she rang back to say that she felt compelled to give me a reading and asked me to travel to her the next day. I did.

I suppose that I was still a little cautious of mediums, because I parked three streets away, so that she couldn't see my car and mention it by way of personal detail. However, when I arrived, she made me feel completely at ease and asked me to wait in a small room in her home, where there were many leaflets and books I could browse. She then called me in... and what she revealed was impossible for anyone outside of my family to know. For me the message given to me was clear: it was time to start working with the spirit world.

She even refused to take payment, for as she said, the spirits were telling her she could not accept payment from one of their own.

Many people were now beginning to talk more openly about spirits, ghosts and the paranormal, and a time of a new awakening was occurring. Television soon got in the act: programmes started being made on these very subjects, and the formation of many paranormal groups also began. I formed my own such group, the 'Bassetlaw Ghost Research Group', where like-minded people who desire to learn more about spirits, ghosts and other paranormal phenomena could meet and investigate together.

7

Conducting an Investigation

So you've read some books and got some of the basic equipment needed for your own paranormal investigation. You've got your eye on a reputedly haunted location and rustled up some colleagues with an interest in things paranormal, sceptical or otherwise. What next?

First of all, it's vitally important that you contact those responsible for the location. Gaining full permission is paramount if you are going to conduct investigations without fear of being arrested for trespassing! I suggest that you write to the owners or occupiers in the first instance, explaining who you are and that you would like to conduct an investigation into alleged paranormal activity at their property and how many team members will be there with you. I would also advise that you offer to provide a copy of your investigation report once it is completed. Be polite and, if your request is declined, accept the decision gracefully. You must never try to change their minds. This will only give you and your group a bad name, which is the last thing you want at such an early stage in your career as a paranormal investigator.

Always try to meet the owners or occupiers, so you can allay any concerns they may have. You must be willing to accept reasonable ground rules put forward prior to your investigation – it is important to have trust on both sides when conducting paranormal research.

PRELIMINARY RESEARCH

Once permission for your investigation has been granted, you can begin the groundwork needed before any activity takes place. A large part of this involves research and information gathering. It is always an advantage if you can delve into the history of the location you have chosen to investigate, as this will give you an opportunity to uncover any events that may give you vital clues as to why it is haunted. It may even help bring to light *what* it is that's supposedly haunting the building.

Your notes from this stage of the process will prove useful at the next stage of the groundwork – interviews!

Interviewing Witnesses

You need to find and interview as many witnesses as you can to discuss any alleged paranormal activity at your chosen location. The purpose of this is to give yourself as much precise and specific information as possible about what has been experienced and when. This sort of information will help you to build a database, which you can refer to when necessary. I've included a template for a witness interview at the back of the book, so you can get an idea as to what sort of questions to ask (see page 124). Any descriptions that your witnesses are able to give during the interview, particularly if they've had a visual encounter, can be researched afterwards.

Location Evaluation and Baseline Tests

The next step is to compile a report evaluating your chosen location and undertake a series of baseline tests at the site. A location evaluation report basically details the overall condition of the place that you are going to investigate. Walk around making notes that detail things like squeaky floorboards; draughty windows and doors; windows and doors that do not shut properly and that may come open during an investigation; noisy pipes and central heating; and any obvious electrical appliances that may interfere with an EMF device. Do this in every area of the building or plot that you are planning to investigate.

PREVIOUS: *Experiments are highly recommended during any paranormal investigation. Here I am drawing around a trigger object experiment – one of the most popular experiments used in paranormal investigation.*

BELOW: *Selecting a setting on a Tri-Field EMF meter, prior to conducting the baseline tests.*

BELOW: *Conducting a 'sweep' of a reputedly haunted aircraft hangar with the EMF meter.*

OPPOSITE: *(Left to right) Nick Scrimshaw, Vince Draper and Simon Deacon discuss the upcoming investigation at the Galleries of Justice, Nottingham – reputedly one of the most haunted locations in England.*

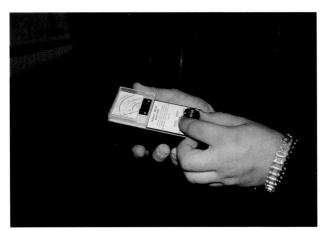

However, if you are undertaking an investigation outside then you need to adapt your evaluation accordingly – EMF readings will be helpful just in case there are any overhead power lines or subterranean power cables that could interfere with your investigation.

Baseline tests are performed to give paranormal investigators a set of default measurements that can be used as a guide during the investigation. These might include a set of temperature readings; measurements detailing humidity and air pressure and EMF data. Remember that the best way to use an EMF meter is to slowly and smoothly 'sweep' the area under investigation from left to right and up and down, taking care to make a note of any electrical devices that may give false readings.

It is certainly beneficial to gather information about the prevailing weather conditions, particularly if the area you are investigating is outside. It may also be useful to know what phase the moon will be in during your investigation, not because I'm suggesting you chase werewolves, but because some reports seem to suggest a slight increase in paranormal phenomena during the different lunar phases.

Starting Your Investigation

Once your preliminary research has been completed you're ready to start the investigation. It's worth mentioning that although it can be advantageous, it is not compulsory to conduct your investigations at night, as plenty of daytime investigations into the paranormal have yielded interesting results. In fact, most investigations take place at night because it makes access to some locations easier, especially if the site is commonly used during daytime hours. What is important, and I can't stress this enough, is that you have obtained permission to conduct the investigation, regardless of the time of day!

Okay, so you've assembled a team of enthusiasts and you've arrived at your chosen location – what now?

Designating a crew room is an important part of any investigation, as this is where members of your team can take a break and generally relax a little when necessary. It's advisable to ensure that you and your team-mates take regular breaks during the investigation, as you need to remain alert and not allow yourself to become too tired. Establishing a base at one particular spot means that you know where your team members are going to be when they are not actively involved in the investigation. This will

help to eliminate false alarms that might be caused by team members wandering about the site.

Before the investigation begins, a set of ground rules needs to be laid down, which everyone on the team should agree to adhere to. For example:

- When taking a break, members must use the crew room and not wander around the site.
- Every individual should be as quiet as possible, whispering only when necessary.
- Members of the team must not smoke or drink alcohol during the investigation.
- Each individual must remain within his or her assigned investigation area unless there is an emergency.
- Everybody should ensure that they know where the emergency exits are situated.

As mentioned earlier (see page 37), if you are splitting your group into smaller teams (something that I recommend if your group is large or the location is of a decent size) each group should have a walkie-talkie. This way you stay in contact with the rest of the group; you can question any strange occurrences with each other in real time; and you will be able control break times.

If you split your team into smaller groups, try to ensure that nobody is investigating alone. It's always better to have somebody else with you to verify – or not, as the case may be – any phenomena that may have been experienced.

The next step is for the group to discuss what the investigation is going to involve and, if necessary, place the groups in different spots throughout the location. Make sure once more that everyone understands the

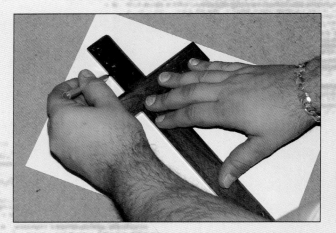

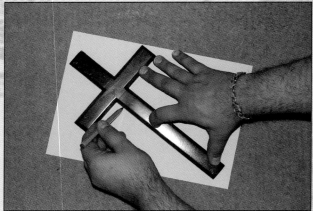

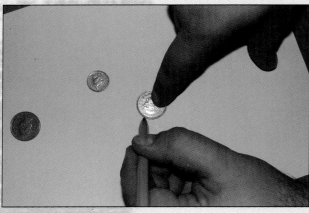

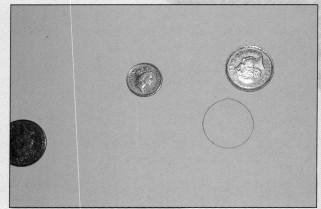

TOP LEFT: *Place your chosen trigger object onto a piece of plain paper, in the area that is subject to supposed paranormal activity, making sure that the surface chosen is flat and sturdy and that all team members know where it is.*

TOP RIGHT: *Holding the trigger object firmly, draw around it.*

ABOVE LEFT & RIGHT: *If a trigger object then gets moved, it can be clearly seen, as in this sequence.*

ground rules and knows what they are about to do. There is no need to allocate a specific job to each individual, as everybody should, more or less, be doing similar things anyway – remaining quiet, moving as little as possible and making notes on anything that they see, hear, sense or smell. The latter is very important as it is one of the basic rules of good investigation technique. If possible everyone should have a basic set of equipment at their disposal, consisting of a notepad and pencil, a small torch with spare batteries and a watch so that significant points in time can be detailed. A dictaphone or cassette recorder

and a 35-mm camera will be beneficial for each of group.

Setting Up Experiments

If you are going to set up any experiments then now is the time to do so. Experiments are highly recommended – you may be surprised by some of the results. As with all aspects of paranormal research, patience is a virtue. The results of experiments are few and far between but, if you persevere, you will eventually be rewarded!

So what kind of experiments would I suggest? Well the first one involves trigger objects (see page 37) and its aim

TOP LEFT: *Another trigger object experiment – this time using flour sieved onto a flat baking tray. This is particularly useful in a location where you cannot ordinarily sieve flour (or talcum powder) freely, such as a historic or important building.*

TOP RIGHT: *With the flour covering the tray, carefully place your objects onto its surface. If they are moved there will be tell-tale tracks, indicating the direction of movement.*

ABOVE LEFT: *Using a 'locked-off' camera can be a great experiment. Simply place a video camera onto a suitable, steady surface and leave it to film. (Again, make sure your crew knows where it is.)*

ABOVE RIGHT: *Here Stuart Edmonds sets up a locked-off camera, ready to film the grounds of Tutbury Castle.*

is to provoke some kind of interaction with whatever may be haunting the location under investigation. The trigger object is placed in the area that is supposed to be active or where paranormal activity has been witnessed. It is a good idea to place the item on a piece of white paper and draw an outline around it. This makes it fairly easy to see if a trigger object has moved, because if it is dislodged from its position the outline will indicate as such.

Small bells are also useful. They can be placed around the site under investigation and provide an audible alert if they are even slightly moved, which is helpful if you happen to be in another area at the time. They can easily be strung across doorways or corridors using cotton or thin string.

Of course, if you are using a trigger object that moves freely, such as a marble or toy car, you will find it fairly awkward to draw around, let alone keep it from moving about as you do so. The best thing to do in this case is to place the object onto finely sprinkled flour or talcum powder – you'll get an even finer dusting if you use a sieve. I actually prefer using flour in this situation, as even unscented talcum powder seems to have a faint perfume, which could prove misleading. However, the choice is yours as the physical results are exactly the same.

To set up the experiment, simply sieve the flour or talcum powder onto your chosen surface (I find it easier and certainly less messy to take a thin metal baking tray with me for this particular purpose) and gently place your trigger object on top of it. Make sure that it is a fairly thick layer of flour or talcum powder and be certain to cover the surface thoroughly. This is helpful for two reasons: first, the object won't move about without some kind of force being applied to it. Second, you won't misinterpret any visible surface that shows through the flour or talcum powder as some kind of paranormal interference – and people have been daft enough to do this!

Once you have set up your trigger object experiment, create a controlled environment by closing off the area in which it is taking place for a specified period of time. To be certain that no tampering occurs, and to stand a chance of capturing any paranormal events, install a video camera to film the trigger object, ensuring that the view is wide enough to capture the object and immediate area around it. Once your investigation is complete, you will be able to see if your object has been disturbed, because there will be telltale trails in the flour or talcum powder to indicate the direction of movement.

If you do use flour or talcum powder on surfaces during your investigations, please seek permission to do so beforehand. Remember that you must always respect the property of others and clean up any kind of mess you've made at the end of your investigation.

You can also sprinkle flour or talcum powder on the floor to try to capture ghostly footsteps. Only use this particular type of experiment on solid surfaces, for example stone or wooden floors, and again seek permission prior to doing so. Do not use this method on carpeted surfaces: the cleaning bill could cost you thousands!

Recording Sound

Using a cassette recorder or dictaphone in a haunted location can provide interesting results. Try to place a device like this in the centre of the supposedly haunted area, as this will give you the best all-round range for capturing any audible noise and can be analysed once the investigation is over.

If you decide to use a recording device in the vicinity of an active investigation area, then remember to remain quiet at all times. If you do happen to make a noise that could be picked up by the cassette recorder then always announce it. This way whoever listens to the recording when the evidence is being analysed will know immediately that it was caused by a living person and not some long-dead entity! You would be truly amazed at just how many individuals involved in paranormal investigations have inadvertently made a noise that was then mistaken as paranormal in nature, only for that individual to later realize that they made the sound when they walked into a door or table (or harpsichord in my case).

Using a cassette recorder or digital dictaphone is also one of the best ways of recording an Electronic Voice Phenomenon (or 'EVP' for short). EVP is the term given to noises captured on recording devices that appear to be discarnate or paranormal in origin. The best method of capturing these sounds is to simply start your recording device and take a leisurely walk through the location under investigation. Some people will say that it is a good idea to engage whatever might be haunting the location in conversation, as this provides something for the ghost or spirit to react to. Whether you decide to talk or not, the choice is yours.

The one thing I will say about recording EVPs is that you should listen very carefully to your recorded audio when

OPPOSITE: *Another useful experiment is to place a small, digital dictaphone in an area of suspected paranormal activity, and leave it on record.*

ABOVE: *Try walking around the investigation area and asking questions – you may be surprised at some of the results. Careful analysis is always needed for any EVP recording.*

analysing it, as more often than not these sounds appear to be very faint and high pitched, a bit like a vinyl album being played at single speed – if you remember those then that's great, if not, ask your parents!

As I mentioned earlier, always try to set up your chosen experiments under controlled conditions. For instance, once the chosen experiment has been set, whether it's a dusting of flour or a sound recording, make as sure as you can that nobody enters the area in which the equipment is positioned. If you can, block access to the room in which the experiment is being held, as this will help eliminate accidental human interference and make any evidence gathered more tangible.

Photographing Ghosts

If you have a camera, whether it's digital or film, then the best way of taking photographs at a haunted location appears to be using gut instinct. When investigators who have captured some kind of apparent paranormal anomaly or activity on camera are then asked why they took the photograph at that precise moment, most of them seem to reply that they sensed or felt that it was the right time to do

so. Some of the best photographs of supposed ghosts have been taken instinctively, so if you feel the need to shoot an image, then snap away. You never know what you'll get.

If you're shooting on film, it doesn't really matter if you use colour or black and white – ghosts don't seem to have a preference. However, make sure you use a high-speed film, as this might give you better results. Whether using film or digital a flash is advisable in darkened conditions, unless, of course, you like taking photos of nothing! If you are processing a 35-mm film, then ask the technicians at the developing lab not to correct or touch-up any of the film and to include all the shots on the roll – even those that appear to have nothing on them.

I could go on to mention all manner of technical specifications regarding the best settings for your camera (assuming that you can alter them in the first place), but I won't. The best thing to do is go out and experiment, find a setting that you are happy with and that you think will give you good results. At the end of the day it's a matter of personal taste, as everyone's initial interpretation of a photograph is different and some people see details in an image that another person finds hard to make out.

8

Investigation Reports

This chapter will highlight a few of the investigations that I have conducted over the years, and that I would like to share with you. At the end of each investigation report I shall throw down some of the questions raised from events that took place during the investigation itself, questions that I think will probably be going through your mind as you read the accounts.

The locations, from which these particular investigation reports come from, range from a 12th-century manor house to a 19th-century Gothic mansion! As I have said in previous chapters, as with all paranormal reports that you may read, please feel free to draw your own conclusions and theories.

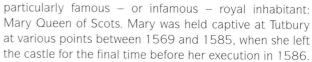

TUTBURY CASTLE, STAFFORDSHIRE, ENGLAND, 2005
EMF reading: 0
Outside temperature: 8°C
Inside temperature: 15°C, dropping to 11°C
Weather conditions: Dry and overcast with a very light breeze
Start time: 11.45 pm

Tutbury Castle is one of the most haunted historical buildings in England. It was once a magnificent structure and dates back hundreds of years, some of which were peaceful and others very turbulent. The castle has seen many a royal and historical figure pass through its doors, but I suppose it is probably best known for one particularly famous – or infamous – royal inhabitant: Mary Queen of Scots. Mary was held captive at Tutbury at various points between 1569 and 1585, when she left the castle for the final time before her execution in 1586.

If, as some people speculate, our emotions somehow imprint themselves onto the materials in the environment that surround us, then Mary Queen of Scots would provide a fascinating example of this theory. She apparently hated her time at Tutbury Castle with a passion.

Mary's ghost is just one of several spirits that are reputed to haunt the castle and its grounds. Dressed in a black gown, the doomed queen has often been seen walking across the lawn at the front of the castle. Other ghosts that frequent Tutbury Castle include a cavalier, who haunts the King's Bedchamber; a monk, who has been spotted wandering in the grounds and on the battlements; a castle guard, who stops people at the main gate; a little blonde child, who has been seen running through the castle itself; and an elderly woman, who has been glimpsed floating outside the window of the Great Hall, possibly walking on a part of the castle that no longer exists but did at some point in the past.

Other strange incidents that have been reported and experienced at Tutbury include people fainting in the King's Bedchamber;

PREVIOUS: *Candle-lit vigils can be atmospheric, even more so if you are in a Torture Chamber like the one at Tutbury Castle, Staffordshire!*

LEFT: *The main façade of Tutbury Castle. The main window (upper middle) is where the shadowy form of an old lady has been seen, floating outside.*

people being touched by something or someone that isn't visible; strange smells; and voices speaking in foreign tongues, which have been heard in the area that once housed the torture chamber.

Accompanying me for the Tutbury investigation were paranormal enthusiasts Nick Scrimshaw, Chris Fryer, Laura Smith, Al Smith and Charlotte Drew. There was nobody else at the castle that night. Our crew room for this investigation was upstairs in the Great Hall. We began the proceedings at approximately 11 pm and used the following investigation equipment:

- 3 digital video cameras with night-vision function
- 2 digital stills cameras
- 2 EMF meters
- 1 tape recorder
- 1 digital voice recorder
- 2 motion detector units
- 1 infra-red thermometer
- 4 walkie-talkies
- 3 digital thermometers
- Trigger objects
- Torches
- Spare batteries

Once everything was in position, Chris and I walked through the castle interior, closing any doors that needed to be secured. These included the door to the café and gift shop on the ground floor, which we had to padlock, a task that was tricky and took some time to complete. Once this was done, we joined the rest of the team who were waiting for us in the crew room, the Great Hall.

At approximately 11.45 pm the team ventured outside to conduct a sweep of the castle grounds, including the folly and the North Tower – the latter is reputed to be the haunt of a white lady. This took roughly 30 minutes and, apart from the odd screech from the Tutbury peacocks – an unnerving sound in the dead of night – the walk passed without incident. With that we returned to the Great Hall.

At 12.30 am, the group split into two smaller teams to conduct the next set of vigils, with Charlotte, Al and Laura taking the King's Bedchamber, and Chris, Nick and me taking the Great Hall, both on upper floors of the castle. Once everyone was in place, silence fell on Tutbury Castle. However, this did not last for long.

THE EQUIPMENT WAS USED AS FOLLOWS:

- One trigger object was set up on paper in the Great Hall with a digital video camera focused on it.

- Another trigger object was set up on paper in the King's Bedchamber, along with a set of motion detectors positioned in such a way as to afford the best possible coverage of the room.

- The cassette recorder was set up to record in the kitchen area on the ground floor.

- The digital voice recorder was set up to record in the main entrance hall.

- The motion detectors were positioned on the stairs leading to the Great Hall.

- The remaining video cameras were 'hand-held' (that is to say they were mobile, not static on a tripod).

- The digital stills cameras were used throughout the investigation and notes taken throughout the night.

After a few moments, a distinctive clicking noise was heard downstairs. I went down to investigate, but nothing out of the ordinary was revealed, so I returned to the Great Hall.

Meanwhile, in the King's Bedchamber, Charlotte, Laura and Al had all experienced cold spots and had taken several photographs that were later found to contain possible light anomalies. Sadly, the ghostly cavalier did not put in an appearance during that vigil.

After 45 minutes both groups reconvened in the Great Hall to discuss their respective vigils and take a break. At this point I quickly checked the experiments and reset the video cameras and cassette recorder. There had been no movement of the trigger objects so far.

At 1.40 am the second set of indoor vigils took place, with the two groups swapping investigation areas. Like the previous group, the team in the King's Bedchamber experienced cold spots, but nothing strange was heard or seen by the group now occupying the Great Hall. After about 45 minutes the team met up again for a brief break to discuss events.

The Puzzle of the Padlock
It was during this break that the most significant event of the investigation occurred. While I was discussing the vigils with the rest of the group, I noticed Charlotte and Laura appear with a tray of drinks. The girls had acquired the drinks tray from the café on the ground floor, so I immediately asked them if they had re-padlocked the door when they left the room. They both looked somewhat confused and told me that the door had already been wide open when they got there.

Those of you who are paying attention will remember that at the beginning of this report I mentioned that it had taken a significant amount of time to padlock this particular door.

It soon became apparent that nobody on the team had opened the door. I went downstairs to check the door for myself and it was clear that if anybody had even attempted to open it, the bolt mechanism would have made a very audible sound, as it was quite difficult to move.

It is sometimes reported that residual energy traces can still be detected in the minutes after a supposed paranormal incident, but EMF readings around the door and in its vicinity showed no increase, nor was there any noticeable drop in temperature. There have also been reports that objects involved in paranormal activity have either felt noticeably warmer or cooler than ambient temperatures, but the padlock was at room temperature. The tape recorder, which was positioned in the kitchen area opposite the café door, was also checked, but it had recorded nothing out of the ordinary.

With the possibility that paranormal activity had taken place – much to everyone's surprise, it has to be said – I decided to install one of the video cameras in a position where it could film the door and padlock, which had been put back into position.

With the camera locked in position, the team proceeded to investigate the castle grounds once more.

OPPOSITE: *An aerial view of Tutbury Castle clearly showing the grounds in which Mary Queen of Scots is said to walk.*

A Strange Shape
At approximately 3.15 am several members of the team saw a dark shape in the distance near the North Tower and torture chamber. The area was investigated and a vigil held, but no further action was witnessed. Digital cameras were used to photograph the object, but nothing could be found that was of a paranormal nature on any of the shots taken during this incident.

With the time now approaching 6 am, we concluded the investigation and decided to get a couple of hours sleep before heading home. During the rest period I was woken several times by yet more noises coming from downstairs. I checked the area thoroughly, but found nothing out of the ordinary.

When the video footage of the padlocked door was reviewed later, I was surprised to hear numerous unidentified sounds on the film, ranging from clicks and bangs to what sounded like faint, distant footsteps and shuffling noises.

Although the investigation at Tutbury Castle proved somewhat inconclusive, it provided some interesting results nonetheless and posed several questions:

1. Who or what had opened the padlocked door?
I know for a fact that the door had been closed and padlocked, as I had performed this task with Chris. I also know for a fact that nobody but my investigation team was present in the castle that night. Lesley Smith, the castle's curator, historian and an authority on Mary Queen of Scots and many other subjects, later told us that this particular incident was not uncommon.

But what was the cause? Several people I have spoken to have suggested that it was the spirit of a castle guard or warden who still insists on doing the rounds, locking or unlocking doors as he may have done during his life at the castle. Who knows?

2. What was the dark shape seen near the North Tower by team members?
Again, there was nobody else at the castle during our investigation. The shape could have been a trick of the light, or lack of it at that time of night, or perhaps it was

FOLLOWING PAGE: *The infamous North Tower at Tutbury, where a dark shape was seen during our investigation.*

the result of tiredness creeping in, although the latter seems unlikely as the team are regulars at these investigations and are quite used to the long hours involved. As mentioned towards the start of this report, there have been numerous sightings of strange figures in the grounds of Tutbury Castle, so perhaps this was another one of them.

3. What was responsible for the noises heard coming from downstairs?

This is another phenomenon that is frequently associated with Tutbury Castle. The area was checked after the noises were heard, but nothing unusual was discovered. There were a number of electrical appliances situated in the kitchen area, but these emitted regular sounds that were exactly the same each time they were produced, so they were easily eliminated as the strange noises that were heard that night.

Unexplained noises and sounds are among the most commonly experienced paranormal phenomena that are associated with reputedly haunted locations, so does the fact that I wasn't able to come up with an explanation for the noises heard mean that they were from a source that was paranormal in nature?

4. Where were the cold spots coming from in the King's Bedchamber?

The answer that automatically springs to mind is that there was a draught entering the room from a window or door.

However, while this rational explanation is entirely possible, it is not very likely, as there was only a light breeze noticeable on the night of the investigation and the cold spots were experienced at certain very localized points within the room itself. You would also expect any draught to be fairly consistent, but this was certainly not the case within the King's Bedchamber. Was it possible that one of the ghostly inhabitants of the castle – the cavalier, the small child, the old woman or even Mary Queen of Scots herself – was trying to make their presence known?

We have to remember that this room has hosted some pretty strange experiences over the years, including cold spots, which have been experienced by numerous individuals on many different occasions.

Tutbury Castle had provided some extremely useful data, and I resolved to visit the site again for a further investigation (see pages 73–77).

THE EDINBURGH VAULTS, SCOTLAND, 2005
EMF reading: 0
Outside temperature: 15°C
Inside temperature: 12°C
Weather conditions: Warm, humid and clear, with little breeze
Start time: 12.30 am

The Edinburgh Vaults – the very name strikes fear into the hearts of some, and usually for good reason. This location is widely regarded to be one of Scotland's most haunted venues, a place so paranormally active that it has been the subject of many television programmes. The vaults were built in 1785 when Edinburgh's South Bridge was constructed, which comprised 19 huge stone arches. Floors and walls were built beneath the arches to form basic rooms, or vaults, which were initially used to house businesses, workshops and homes. At the turn of the 19th century some of these vaults were filled in and forgotten about until 1980, when they were rediscovered and things really started going bump in the night!

Among the ghostly inhabitants that have been witnessed within the vaults are a stocky man nicknamed 'Mr Boots'; a little boy and a small friendly dog. Other incidents that have been experienced and reported include items of clothing being tugged at, hair being pulled, cold and hot spots, light anomalies and feelings of sadness and anger. With me on this investigation were Nick Scrimshaw and several guest investigators, and the equipment used during this investigation included:

• 2 digital video cameras with night-vision function and tripods
• 2 digital stills cameras
• 2 EMF meters
• 2 digital voice recorders
• 2 infra-red thermometers (hand-held)
• 3 digital thermometers
• 2 trigger objects
• 2 motion detectors

The team was divided into two smaller groups and we ventured down the winding staircase that led to the vaults. After a brief familiarization period, the two groups occupied the chosen vigil areas for the first 40-minute

THE EQUIPMENT WAS USED AS FOLLOWS:

• One digital video camera fixed on a tripod was initially set up in the main vault. It was set up in each vault at some point during the investigation.

• Another digital video camera was hand-held.

• The two EMF meters were hand-held.

• One digital voice recorder was positioned in the main vault.

• The other digital voice recorder was positioned in vault number 8 – reputedly the most paranormally active vault of all – with a trigger object set up on paper.

• One trigger object was positioned in the rear vault corridor.

• One of the motion detectors was used in various areas throughout the night, but initially installed in the main vault known as the wine cellar.

• The digital thermometers were positioned at various points throughout the vaults and periodically checked. Each had a memory function to record minimum/maximum temperatures reached. (N.B. It is widely thought that rapid fluctuations in temperature of +/- 5°C could be indicative of paranormal activity, but this is open to interpretation.)

• The digital stills cameras were used throughout the investigation.

LEFT: *The exit from the main vault. People have reported seeing a figure standing in the blocked-off area above the doorway.*

BELOW LEFT: *The area inside the Edinburgh Vaults, known as the Wine Cellar. Here the ghost of a little boy nicknamed 'Jack' has been seen... and felt!*

OPPOSITE: *The séance room where one investigator almost fainted, 'Jack' made his presence known and the emotions of one investigator took a dramatic turn for the worse.*

watch. My group was holding a vigil in the main vault and the rooms immediately adjacent to it; Nick and his team were conducting a vigil in the remaining vaults. Apart from the occasional noise heard by my team, which in all honestly sounded like someone's stomach rumbling, nothing of note happened. After the allotted time was up the groups swapped positions.

Again not much seemed to happen. After the 45-minute period was complete, we took a break to discuss what little, if any, paranormal activity had taken place. Several light anomalies had been captured on various digital cameras during the first vigil.

A Spooky Séance
After the break, we renewed our attempts to discover paranormal phenomena and headed back towards the vaults. Some of my group wished to participate in a séance, to which I agreed, but only after confirming that several members had already had experience of such events and discovering that my team contained two 'sensitives' – individuals who are allegedly more in touch with ghosts and spirits. The two sensitives were to conduct the proceedings. Although I took no part in the séance, I observed the event.

This is when things really began to happen...

The time was approaching 2 am and the séance was in full swing. Suddenly, a commotion came from the group. I quickly flicked on my torch and I could see that a young female member of the séance had fallen over, almost fainting. Having checked that she was uninjured, her partner and I supported her until she regained her breath and her legs had lost their jelly-like consistency.

She was, however, very confused and started to panic, believing that something strange had taken hold of her arm. She calmed down somewhat when I explained to her that I was holding her arm to support her. We took her outside, but she was visibly shaken and slightly tearful. She then began to tell us what had happened.

As the séance began, she felt fine. Then she started to get the sensation that something was pushing her backwards. This continued for a few seconds, until she lost her balance and keeled over in shock and panic.

I must point out that this kind of behaviour is very common at a séance. It is often caused by heightened imaginations, fatigue and lack of food. All of these factors applied in this instance. Ten minutes later the woman was fine and raring to go.

Just as we were about to return to the vaults, we were joined by another team member, who was also distressed and weepy. After comforting her, she began to explain her state. She had felt fine during the vigil she was conducting, and had decided to walk through the vaults to see how other members of the group were getting on. Upon walking into a certain vault, she had become very emotional and had to leave the area quickly, which is why she was outside now. She was soon feeling much better.

Another break was taken, during which I informed everyone that they were under no obligation to continue should they wish to sit out the rest of the night. Everyone decided to carry on with the investigation.

It was now nearing 3.15 am.

A Tactile Spirit?

The group that had conducted the earlier séance was now conducting a follow up in the same area, which was on the far side of the vaults near the wine cellar. After ensuring all was well and that everything was being conducted properly I decided to take a check on the other team members. As I was doing this I noticed the second girl to have become upset earlier was again very agitated.

this was Mr Boots? According to Jack, the nasty spirit was not around at this point.

Things then started to get even more physical, as Jack began to pull and push those he was speaking to forwards and backwards. This continued for a number of minutes, until one of the participants broke away from the group. Her husband quickly came to comfort her, but then to his shock, his wife became aggressive and told him to leave her alone. He tried to comfort her once more, offering his arm to put around her shoulder. Again she responded aggressively.

She was eventually led upstairs and taken outside for some fresh air to help her clear her head. I decided to call a halt to the séance and closed it down in the correct fashion. When asking what had happened during the séance she told me that an overwhelming sense of anger had come over her, which she had attributed to the spirit of a woman – apparently it was Jack's mother.

As this feeling intensified she had broken away from the séance, but still retained the anger when her husband had tried to comfort her. The remainder of the night proved fruitless, and at 6 am it was decided to call it a night and finish the investigation.

The investigation at the Edinburgh Vaults raised several obvious questions:

She told me that something kept touching the top of her head and wouldn't leave her alone. I decided to stay with her for reassurance and we sat in one of the smaller vaults together. After a little while she again complained that something was touching her head and began to become very emotional once more.

I suggested that she tell whatever it was to leave her alone, which she duly did. I also proceeded to tell her that in all my years of paranormal investigating I had not been harmed in any way, shape or form. This seemed to bring her real comfort, and I am pleased to say that the rest of her investigation passed without incident. Back at the second séance, however, things were beginning to heat up a little.

The Second Séance

As I entered the vault where the séance was taking place, two of the participants seemed to be communicating with the spirit of a young boy. Upon asking a question the young spirit responded 'Yes' or 'No' by lowering or raising the participants' hands. They had so far deduced that the little boy was called Jack, that he was five years old and that he knew of at least one other spirit within the vaults, a rather malevolent character who scared him. Perhaps

1. Did the girl who almost fainted during the séance really experience a paranormal episode?

Perhaps she did, or perhaps it could simply be put down to a mixture of overexcitement, a lack of food and an overactive imagination running away with her in the dark conditions and allegedly haunted surroundings? Could the same theory also be applied to the second girl? After all, she did seem to calm down noticeably once I had been able to reassure her.

2. Was the spirit boy, 'Jack', really interacting with the two participants during the séance?

Possibly, and it would seem that the group certainly had a very real experience of some description. But did it have a paranormal origin? Plenty would argue both for and against the possibilities, so who knows? Maybe it was, maybe it wasn't.

3. Was the anger experienced by the séance participant really caused by an angry spirit presence?

I had spoken to both her and her husband prior to the investigation and they had both joined me on a previous investigation at the Galleries of Justice in Nottingham, so I had already seen how both of them reacted under investigation conditions. Also, both of them had actually conducted investigations in the past.

Both of them were perfectly relaxed throughout this investigation and there was no indication that would suggest the outburst was imminent. Immediately after

the séance it was plain that her husband was not only shocked by what had happened, but also very confused, which caused me to think that it was totally unexpected. It would certainly appear that some kind of emotion had overcome her, but where this came from remains a complete puzzle.

Could it be that she had somehow entered an altered state of consciousness during the séance, which allowed a brief connection with the spirit world? As I am always saying, there are parts of the brain that we know nothing about, so it could be possible.

That said, many people who read this would argue that the whole episode was the result of a very vivid imagination, an opinion to which they are quite entitled. Approaching paranormal subjects with an open mind is always advisable. Feel free once more to draw your own conclusions from this report.

BELOW: *A thermometer (*far right*), left in the Wine Cellar to record and monitor any fluctuations that should occur.*

'LOCATION X', NORTH-WEST ENGLAND, 2000
EMF reading: N/A
Outside temperature: 6°C
Inside temperature: 19°C
Weather conditions: Dry and overcast, with a slight mist; very cold
Start time: 11.30 pm

This investigation took place at a site that I shall merely name 'Location X', so as not to cause undue attention to the property. Many people believe this location to be one of the most paranormally active sites in Britain today, if not *the* most active. While I am not in such a position to confirm this, I can certainly say that some rather bizarre incidents did occur during the investigation, which I shall now detail for your perusal.

'Location X' is situated in north-west England and, like so many of this country's magnificent and historically important buildings, it dates back several hundred years. As with Tutbury Castle, it has seen its fair share of both peaceful and violent times. With me for this investigation were Dan Wright, Kerry Wright and Graeme Croft; nobody else was present at the location at the time of our visit. Our designated crew room for the night was the Hall, which was roughly central to the building and afforded us views into other parts of the building and its grounds.

Among the ghosts believed to be haunting this location are several monks, a cavalier, children, a young woman and a phantom cat. Among the incidents that had been reported here were banging noises, footsteps, hair pulling, hand holding, strange smells and various disembodied voices and screams. All these events had been experienced in every room of the building at some point or another.

The following equipment was used during this investigation:

- 2 digital video cameras with tripods
- 3 digital stills cameras
- 1 35-mm SLR camera with infra-red black-and-white film and a filter on the lens
- 2 tape recorders
- 2 digital thermometers (static, not hand-held)
- 2 trigger objects
- 2 walkie-talkies
- Sleeping bags
- Torches and spare batteries
- Notepads and pencils

An Outside Vigil

Having positioned the equipment, I decided that we should start with an investigation of the grounds, which is where ghostly monks have been spotted and where young children have also been seen and heard – playing on the lawn to the front of the property.

We split up into two groups – Dan and Kerry, and Graeme and myself – and set off in opposite directions, torches and walkie-talkies in hand. Once settled, both groups conducted a 20-minute vigil at each end of the grounds.

At 11.45 pm Dan radioed through to me on his walkie-talkie to ask if Graeme or I had broken from our position and started walking around the grounds. I replied that we hadn't and reiterated that we must inform each other prior to any movement. I asked why he was inquiring. Dan replied that he and Kerry had heard someone or something walking past their vigil spot. The incident was then investigated, but nothing out of the ordinary was uncovered.

Nothing else untoward happened during the remainder of the vigil outside, so we headed back into the building. After warming our hands and having a brief chat and a drink we discussed the next vigil areas before heading off on our separate ways. These were the two bedrooms, which had both experienced some rather peculiar incidents.

Into the Bedrooms

It had been said that, within the walls of bedroom two, lay the remains of some poor unfortunate who had been incarcerated many moons ago. Maybe this was true, but who knows? It was certainly one reason that had been offered to explain the supposed paranormal activity that had taken place within this room. One incident that had been reported involved the bedroom door, which had a strange tendency to be suddenly and forcefully closed if left open. The door latch had also been violently shaken, as if some unseen force was trying to make its escape from the room.

Bedroom one was a much more tranquil spot, although it had still been the site of some odd incidents. In this particular room, a young spirit girl had frequently pulled the hair of visitors to the building; on occasion she would also hold their hands or sit on their knees. An interesting scenario, as I'm sure you will agree.

Graeme and I were situated in bedroom two, while Dan and Kerry were in bedroom one. We began a 45-minute vigil at approximately 12.30 am. I wish I could report that Graeme and I witnessed the walled-up corpse making a bid for freedom from within the confines of its wattle and daub prison, but alas we did not. In fact nothing happened, and with 10 minutes of our vigil remaining I left Graeme to bedroom two and joined the proceedings in bedroom one. Once I got there, things started to happen almost immediately.

The first thing that happened was that the band fastening Kerry's hair back was gently raised and lowered again, causing her slight surprise and alarm. I have to say that I love the look on a person's face as they turn around believing one of the group members has just played some kind of prank on them, only to find that the person in question is on the other side of the room – it's priceless!

This incident was promptly followed by a distinct drop in ambient temperature – a fall from 17°C of about 5°C to hover around the 12°C mark. This lasted for approximately three minutes before the temperature returned to normal.

I contacted Graeme in the other bedroom and he confirmed that he had felt no obvious temperature fluctuation. Another couple of minutes passed and Graeme came to complete the team in bedroom one. For the remainder of the vigil all was quiet. At about 1.25 am we took a break for drinks and a quick snack. During the break several unexplained noises were heard, including a metallic click; a faint, yet constant tapping; and a brief creaking noise, which seemed to be emanating from one of the chairs positioned at the table.

THIS EQUIPMENT WAS USED AS FOLLOWS:

- One digital video camera and tripod was set up to film the upper landing, with a view into bedroom two.
- One tape recorder was set up to record in the chapel area, where a trigger object was also placed on paper.
- The other tape recorder was set up to record in bedroom one, along with a trigger object on paper and a digital thermometer.
- The second digital thermometer was positioned in the main entrance hall.
- The third digital thermometer was placed on the main stairwell.
- The other digital video camera was hand-held.
- The digital stills cameras were used continuously throughout the investigation, along with the 35-mm SLR camera.

It could be said that the creaking chair was caused by changes in room temperature, just as floorboards and beams tend to creak and groan in old properties, as the temperature drops and the wood cools down, but the temperature in the Hall hadn't faltered, so this explanation was ruled out.

At this point, I went back upstairs to examine the equipment positioned there and check the experiments. Nothing of note had taken place.

The Shaking Door
I was about to exit bedroom two, when I heard Dan, Kerry and Graeme running up the main stairs in my direction. To say they seemed panicked would be an understatement. I calmed them down before finding out what had happened.

They proceeded to explain that they had been checking the front door to confirm it was locked, but as they did so it shook violently several times. Further research told us that this incident had occurred on a regular basis. It is worth mentioning at this point that this was no ordinary door: it was made of solid oak and dated back several hundred years. It was also locked with numerous large iron bolts. The door was also covered by a security light – a fact that was blatantly obvious upon our arrival at the location, as it half-blinded us as we entered the building. The security light, which would have stayed on for several minutes if someone was present, as it did at our arrival, hadn't even flickered.

The incident had taken the trio by surprise, and they'd bolted upstairs. I immediately went to check the door. After quickly and thoroughly scouring the grounds I was satisfied that there was no-one messing around outside. I returned inside the building, locking the massive oak door behind me. We took another 10-minute break to ensure that everyone had calmed down before resuming the investigation. Nothing further happened until about 3.35 am.

The Squeezed Hand

Dan, Kerry and Graeme were conducting another vigil in bedroom one, where they had been for about 25 minutes. Suddenly Kerry felt something squeeze her hand. This continued for a few moments, but ceased as soon as Kerry tried to lead whatever or whoever was attached to her hand out of the room. It transpired that the same experience had been recorded in this room on numerous occasions. There was yet another noticeable drop in ambient temperature while this incident took place. All three waited a few more moments in the bedroom to see if there would be a repeat of what had just happened, but there was not and with that they made their way back to the Hall, where I was waiting.

Dan started to relate the experience to me, only to be cut short by Kerry herself, who was now crying and becoming somewhat distressed. She eventually began to tell us that as Dan had started to speak she had heard a small child laughing and giggling in the main entrance hall. Nobody else had heard this sound, which is one reason why Kerry was so upset. This was another incident that had been experienced on a number of occasions at Location X.

We comforted Kerry for a few moments or so but, with the time fast approaching 4.30 am, it was decided that we should call an end to the investigation. I reset the cameras and checked on the experiments before heading back to the Hall, grabbing my sleeping bag and joining the others for some rest before we left the site.

However, a number of strange noises made continuous sleep almost impossible. At one point it actually sounded like somebody was walking in the Chapel and there was also a definite sound of cups and crockery being moved that was coming from the kitchen area. Upon investigation, the causes of these noises could not be established.

Looking back at the various possible paranormal incidents that occurred at 'Location X' during the investigation one could surmise that it was quite an active place. But there are a few questions that still remain unanswered to this day.

1. What shook the front door so violently?

There was nobody in the grounds when they were checked and the fact that the security light had not been triggered seemed to back this up. The shaking door is a regularly reported incident, so the possibility that this was paranormal in nature cannot be ruled out.

ABOVE: *Daniel and Kerry Wright – two of the investigators who accompanied me to 'Location X'.*

2. What had touched Kerry's hair and held her hand?
Again, similar incidents have been regularly reported. It has to be said that Kerry comes across as a no-nonsense type of person and, having known her and her husband Dan for a number of years, this is something I can confirm.

Furthermore, she is not someone prone to imagining spooky scenarios, so it is perfectly possible that she was experiencing some kind of genuine paranormal phenomenon.

BELOW: *During the time we conducted the investigation, noises, like those of plates and other kitchen paraphernalia moving, were clearly heard.*

3. What was the source of the child's laughter that Kerry heard?
This is simply inexplicable. Nobody else was present at the location, especially any young children! As mentioned earlier in this report, children have been seen and heard playing on the lawn outside the building, and a little research showed that the sound of children laughing had also been heard inside the property. Is it possible that, because Kerry was the only female on the team, she became the focus or catalyst for whatever haunts 'Location X'? Perhaps, as this sort of thing has been known to happen. But as always you are free to draw your own conclusions about this investigation and all of the incidents reported.

WOODCHESTER MANSION, GLOUCESTERSHIRE, ENGLAND
EMF reading: 0
Outside temperature: -2°C
Inside temperature (average): 2°C
Weather conditions: Bitterly cold and clear, with a light-to-moderate breeze
Start time: 10.30 pm

Situated in the Cotswold county of Gloucestershire, Woodchester Mansion is an interesting location that I had been lucky enough to visit twice before prior to this particular investigation. Both previous visits were undertaken for a the purpose of a television series. Nonetheless, I was really looking forward to a fresh investigation – Woodchester is rapidly gaining a reputation among paranormal enthusiasts as one of the most haunted locations in the UK, and it is a favourite of mine.

Among the phenomena that have been recorded here over the years are the spectral figures of American and Canadian soldiers (both were stationed here during the Second World War); the figure of a Roman Centurion, which has been seen at various points around the grounds of the mansion; and a strange dwarf-like figure, which was spotted outside the building.

In Woodchester's chapel the sound of falling masonry has been heard, but upon inspection no explanation for these noises could be found. Unexplained light anomalies, noises, smells and other shadowy forms have been seen inside the building.

With me for this investigation were Nick Scrimshaw and Vince Draper. We were also joined by several guest investigators, and all were eager to see what they could uncover within Woodchester Mansion's vast and mysterious interior.

The equipment used for this investigation was as follows:

- 2 digital video cameras with night-vision and tripods
- 3 digital still cameras
- 2 digital voice recorders
- 2 EMF meters
- 2 infra-red thermometers
- 2 trigger objects
- 2 digital thermometers
- Torches
- Walkie-talkies
- Spare batteries

We arrived at the site earlier than our planned start time, so that we could take some photographs. The designated crew room for this investigation was the drawing room. As usual the group was divided into several smaller teams: Nick took his team to the second floor, while Vince took the ground floor and chapel, leaving me to take my small group to the

OPPOSITE: *The sombre frontage of Gloucestershire's infamous Woodchester Mansion – reputed to be one of the most haunted buildings in the UK.*

ABOVE: *The table used during the table-tilting experiment. Did the experiment have anything to do with the unexplained noises?*

cellar area. From these positions we started the first set of vigils, lasting for approximately 45 minutes. The team leaders maintained contact via the walkie-talkies.

The Table-Tilting Experiment

Things seemed quiet – almost too quiet. However, after about 30 minutes, two members of my team came running out of the cellar, both of them quite flustered. The pair had been conducting an experiment known as 'table-tilting' – they had placed their hands lightly on the surface of a small table in an attempt to channel energy from any spirit haunting the area, the idea being that the ghost would interact with them by moving the table. Suddenly, they heard a strange noise, which seemed to come from above and behind them. We checked out the area and could find nothing that could have produced the noise; nevertheless, I stayed with the group in the cellar for the remaining 15 minutes of the vigil. Nothing else occurred, and so a brief break was called. This was more than welcome as it gave the team the chance to warm up by an open fire. Woodchester Mansion, in part at least, is

THE EQUIPMENT WAS USED AS FOLLOWS:

- The digital video cameras were hand-held.

- One digital voice recorder was positioned in the cellar area.

- The EMF meters were hand-held.

- The infra-red thermometers were hand-held.

- One trigger object was set up on paper and positioned in the chapel.

- The other trigger object was set up on paper and positioned in the kitchen.

- One digital thermometer was positioned in the cellar.

- The other digital thermometer was positioned in the kitchen.

almost derelict and as such the cold really bites, especially through the windows, which have no glass in them. It was absolutely freezing that night and I would strongly advise that, should you venture to Woodchester Mansion during the winter months, you wear thermals!

Strange Footsteps and a Ghostly Mist

A second set of vigils began 20 minutes later. This time, I took a team to the second floor. Nick's group held a vigil in the cellar and Vince opted for the ground floor and chapel area, where I had previously heard the phantom sounds of falling masonry. During my vigil several light anomalies were caught on camera and several unexplained noises were heard that sounded like something thudding on stone.

Downstairs in the cellar, Nick's team experienced a number of cold breezes that went as suddenly as they had come. The temperature in the cellar also dropped mysteriously by 6°C, only to rise again moments later. Vince's vigil seemed to pass without incident.

At about 1 am it was time to take another break. After that the third set of vigils began. My group took the chapel and ground floor – I hoped to experience some phenomena similar to the crashing masonry that I had experienced two years before. Vince took the cellar and Nick took his team to the first floor.

After 10 minutes or so I decided to wander over to the mansion's original kitchen, where a clock mechanism had been reported to move by unseen means. This proved to be a little disappointing, because the object had been moved back to the clock tower in which it was originally located, but we still decided to hold a vigil in this area for a few moments before continuing our meander through the ground floor rooms and corridors. At this point I split up from my team and walked to the area where the workmen's tools are kept. I had only been there for about 30 seconds when I heard somebody walking up behind me. I turned around, expecting to see another member of the team and was quite taken aback to see nobody there! As you could imagine this sent a shiver down my spine and after a few seconds, which felt like forever, I started looking around for the nearest team members, who were

OPPOSITE: *Woodchester Mansion's eerie cellar. Some people believe that the practice of 'Dark Arts' was undertaken here.*

in the kitchen about 20 metres or so away. I asked if anyone had heard or seen anybody walking around, but they had not heard a thing.

Meanwhile, Nick had done some wandering of his own and was now on the ground floor with me. He was taking pictures in the room directly opposite the main staircase and this yielded some surprising and interesting results. Several of the images revealed an unexplained mist. Through a process of elimination, Nick ruled out any rational causes, such as breathing, condensation or fog on the lens. As yet the causes remain unknown. The rest of the vigil passed without incident.

Glasswork

During the next break it was interesting to hear that many of the individuals involved seemed to have experienced some form of paranormal activity or other, primarily in the form of light anomalies. Once everyone was refreshed and warm, the next set of vigils took place. I decided to take a roaming role during this period and eventually found my way into the cellars, where a small team was conducting an experiment called glasswork. They had placed their fingertips on an upturned glass on a tabletop in the hope of getting any spirit forces that may be present to interact with them by moving the object across the surface of the table in answer to questions. I do not take part in exercises such as glasswork or table-tilting, purely because physical contact with the items is involved. As such you cannot completely control the environment in which you are undertaking the experiment because it is not possible to rule out accidental human interaction with the objects. However, everybody has their own opinion about these matters and it may be useful to take part in such experiments, provided that they are supervised and conducted by individuals who are experienced and knowledgeable in these methods of spirit communication.

The team had succeeded in getting the glass to move, which resulted in some excitement. I left them to it, as Nick had just contacted me on his walkie-talkie. He was on the second floor and had some interesting news to impart. He had been sitting in the passage that led to the room where tools were stored, which is where I had earlier held a vigil. After a period of around 3–4 minutes he heard someone walking about nearby – just as I had experienced earlier.

He switched on his torch immediately and shone it in the direction of the noises. He thought he saw something disappearing around a corner at the end of the corridor. I asked whether it could have been an animal, for example a cat, but he estimated that the shape was at least 4 feet in height – clearly far too big to be a domestic moggie! Nothing was found when we investigated the scene. This kind of sighting has been reported before at Woodchester Mansion, although nobody is certain who or what it is.

The end of our investigation was fast approaching, so we decided to wrap up – quite literally as it was *still* freezing – and call it a night. However, the investigation had posed some very intriguing questions.

1. What was the mist that appeared on several photos taken by Nick?

Well it would be easy to dismiss this incident as somebody's breath caught on camera, if it wasn't for the fact that Nick tried to reproduce the effect by breathing out and taking a photograph several times. He even asked somebody else to do the same, without success. He also wiped the camera lens, to rule out the effects of condensation and even held his breath when taking the shot to ensure he ruled this out. It is interesting to note that on more than one occasion he

ABOVE: *The ghostly mist that was captured by Nick during the investigation at Woodchester Mansion, and remains unexplained.*

OPPOSITE: *Stuart Edmonds armed with a night-vision camera, ready for action. Here he waits for the spirits of Bodelwyddan Castle to make his acquaintance.*

was actually pointing the camera towards the ceiling when the mist was captured. Ghostly mists are not uncommon in haunted locations.

2. What had Nick and I heard in the corridor?

These incidents were most peculiar, especially as I didn't see anything when I first heard the sounds, whereas Nick swears that he saw something. But does the fact that I didn't see anything mean that Nick must have imagined it? Of course not.

I am the first to admit that I am about as receptive to psychic or paranormal phenomena as a house brick! So just because I don't see things that doesn't mean that others on the team can't. Needless to say, upon checking and making certain that other members were not in the area when Nick saw the shape, we cannot come to any definite conclusions about what had been encountered.

TUTBURY CASTLE, STAFFORDSHIRE, ENGLAND, SECOND INVESTIGATION, 2005

EMF reading: 0
Outside temperature: 12°C
Inside temperature: 18°C
Weather conditions: Cold and dry with clear skies
Start time: 10.30 pm

As detailed in the report that covers the previous visit to Tutbury Castle (see pages 54–57), some rather odd incidents had occurred during our investigation at the site – the padlocked door incident; the various unexplained noises captured on video and the mysterious shape or figure seen near the North Tower. And so I was absolutely delighted to be given the chance to undertake a follow-up investigation in the hope of encountering further paranormal activity.

With me on the return visit to Tutbury was a team that comprised Nick Scrimshaw, Vince Draper and Stuart Edmunds. We arrived at the site with plenty of time in hand to explore areas of interest and discuss the routine for the night ahead. As on the previous investigation, the designated crew-room was to be the Great Hall. The investigation was due to begin at 10.30 pm.

THIS EQUIPMENT WAS USED AS FOLLOWS:

- One trigger object was set up in the King's Bedchamber, with a video camera focused it.

- Another trigger object was set up on paper in the Torture Chamber area next to the North Tower; one digital voice recorder was also set up in the same location.

- One video camera was trained on the padlocked door (see page 56).

- The second digital voice recorder was set up in the Great Hall.

- The third digital voice recorder was set up in the Torture Chamber.

- The remaining cameras, infra-red thermometers and EMF meters were all hand-held, and were used extensively throughout the investigation.

The following investigation equipment was used during the investigation:
- 3 digital video cameras
- 4 digital still cameras
- 3 EMF meters
- 2 digital voice recorders
- 2 infra-red thermometers
- 2 walkie-talkies
- 2 digital thermometers
- Trigger objects
- Torches
- Spare batteries
- Notepad and pencils
- 2 tripods

ABOVE: *The North Tower, Tutbury Castle. Below this imposing stone tower is the Torture Chamber, home to numerous strange incidents and where the light was seen by Nick and Stuart.*

across the castle grounds. From our vantage point on the South Tower, we were also able to see the North Tower clearly, where the unidentifiable black shape or figure had been observed on our previous investigation at Tutbury.

After about 20 minutes into our vigil on the South Tower, and with our cameras constantly snapping away, we experienced our first unexpected occurrence of the night – the door at the bottom of the tower slammed shut! Alas this was merely because the wind had suddenly picked up, but it was enough to send a shot of adrenaline racing through everyone's veins. The only other thing that happened while we were standing on the South Tower was that my torch picked up two tiny eyes peering out of the darkness at the base of the castle perimeter. However, these weren't supernatural in origin – they just belonged to a little black cat on a quest for a late night snack of the furry kind.

The Vigil in the Torture Chamber

After almost a whole hour of being exposed to the elements on the South Tower, a break was called so we could all warm up a little bit. Back inside the castle we discussed the next area for investigation – the Torture Chamber. I was particularly looking forward to exploring this spot, as some bizarre incidents had occurred there.

The team stayed together for the first half of the investigation, which included a group vigil on top of the South Tower. From this vantage point we had a great view of almost all of the castle grounds, so we scanned the area for any possible signs of strange activity – after all the spectral figure of Mary, Queen of Scots is said to glide

On one particular night a candle had been left burning in the room after it had been locked and secured for the day. When the torture chamber was reopened the next day it was revealed that something quite inexplicable had taken place – a manuscript that had been left in the room had been burned to ashes, but the candle had been positioned on the opposite side of the room! As if this wasn't strange enough, another candle had mysteriously appeared. This room was also the place where strange, possibly foreign voices had been heard on occasion. So with these tales in mind, the team marched over to the Torture Chamber at about midnight to begin the next vigil. We stayed at this site for roughly an hour, but the vigil proved rather disappointing and nothing of note was reported. Another break ensued.

During the break I checked on the trigger objects and inserted new tapes into the video cameras. None of the trigger objects had moved. At about 1.45 am the team split into two groups: I was with Vince in the Great Hall and King's Bedchamber, while Nick and Stuart decided to investigate the Torture Chamber and the grounds. The teams maintained contact via walkie-talkie.

With the lights out inside the castle, Vince and I sat quietly, listening for anything that might be out of the ordinary. After 10 minutes or so had elapsed, Vince, who was positioned at the opposite end of the hall to me, asked me if I could hear anything untoward from where I was standing. At this point I listened more intently and sure enough I could hear a faint noise coming from downstairs. It sounded like furniture being moved, although I did not say anything to Vince to avoid the possibility of auto-suggestion, which is when an idea or thought is inadvertently placed in another person's mind. For instance, if I said to you that I could hear a dog barking it would plant the thought in your mind and you would think you had heard it, even though you quite possibly hadn't. Make sense? Good. Try it with your friends and see how many of them you can catch out, it is quite amusing when they become convinced of something that never happened just because you have suggested it to them. Anyway, back to the investigation.

I asked Vince what he thought he had heard. He'd heard the same as I had – the sound of furniture being dragged around downstairs. However, there was nobody downstairs. The noises continued for a few moments then stopped. Upon investigating the area, it was found

that nothing had been moved at all and after a thorough search of the area we repositioned ourselves in the Great Hall. Just five minutes later the walkie-talkie came alive: it was Nick. He wanted to know if either Vince or I had been outside at all, particularly in the vicinity of their vigil. We had not, and asked why he wanted to know.

From within the Torture Chamber Nick and Stuart had seen what looked like a torch shining underneath the door from the outside. Both had the distinct sensation that somebody was on the other side. As they relayed this information to the two of us in the Great Hall, I ran over to the front window to get a clear view of the Torture Chamber and the North Tower – whatever it was, it was definitely not there now. Unfortunately, Stuart's video camera ran out of tape just moments before the incident took place.

After checking outside the Torture Chamber once more, Nick and Stuart joined us in the Great Hall for a brief respite so that we could discuss what had just occurred. I cannot emphasize enough how important it is

BELOW: *The view from one of the North Tower's windows. Here you can see the folly that was reputedly built on top of an oubliette, still full of its unfortunate victims.*

ABOVE: *The windswept South Tower, where our first vigil of the night took place. The slamming door can be clearly seen (*fourth archway from the left, ground level*).*

to take regular refreshment breaks during investigations into the paranormal. It gives your eyes time to relax after staring into the dark for prolonged periods and keeps your body topped up with fluids. Don't forget that most of us are used to sleeping from about 11 pm!

It was now about 3.15 am and after another vigil of approximately 30 minutes we decided to call it a night and get some rest before our journey home. Vince and Nick opted to sleep in the Great Hall, leaving Stuart and myself to take our slumber within the King's Bedchamber. A door connecting the King's Bedchamber and the Great Hall was left ajar as to afford the quickest entry – or exit – to either area.

We slept with our cameras poised and ready to click into action at the first opportunity. However, the night passed without incident – or so we thought.

Strange Stirrings While Asleep

At about 9 am we began to stir and started to pack up our equipment. As we did so, Nick casually asked Stuart and myself who had been walking up and down the stairs in the King's Bedchamber in the early hours of the morning. Puzzled, we turned to Nick and informed him almost simultaneously that neither of us had done so.

Nick then told us that during the night he had heard someone – or something – walking around on the stairs situated in the King's Bedchamber. He had assumed, much to his regret, that it was either Stuart or me filming on the stairs. And so, without giving the footsteps a second thought, he'd returned to his slumber.

To this day, Nick still kicks himself for not investigating those footsteps, but even the best investigators are sometimes caught out. Anyway, the fact remains that neither Stuart nor I had heard anything at all while sleeping in the room, something that still perplexes us today. After all, we were only a matter of feet away from the staircase, which was the source of the noises.

Upon checking the video footage, audio recordings and cameras, I was surprised to find that nothing at all out of the ordinary had been captured. Nevertheless, the investigation threw up some interesting questions.

1. What had been seen outside the door of the Torture Chamber during Nick and Stuart's vigil?

This has got me stumped to be honest. As you will recall I looked over to the Torture Chamber from my position in the Great Hall – it was an uninterrupted view from this vantage point. I could not see anyone or anything, especially a light source of any description.

So do we dismiss this straight away? Well depending on what theory you might apply to the situation, no. Had Nick and Stuart somehow managed to perhaps enter an altered mental state, which allowed them to briefly 'see' something that I could not? Or had optimum atmospheric conditions perhaps produced a playback of some kind, rather like a cinematic projection of an event that happened long ago in the area where they conducted their vigil? Such an incident could have been so brief that it ceased by the time I moved over to the window in the Great Hall to take a look.

Perhaps it is possible that one of the above did occur, but bear in mind that these explanations are theoretical and as such we cannot rely on them for a definitive answer. All I can say is that I know both of the individuals who witnessed this particular incident well, and I would say that neither of them are prone to imagining things during investigations. Both are experienced team members and think rationally about any experiences they may have before coming to any conclusions.

2. What were the noises heard by Vince and me whilst in the Great Hall?

Again this is confusing. The noises definitely came from beneath the Great Hall, but when the area was inspected nothing untoward was found. This is a common incident at Tutbury Castle. Had we somehow tuned into events from another period when furniture and other objects were being shifted about? Auto-suggestion can be ruled out as an explanation as far as I am concerned, because neither Vince nor I had actually put a name or origin to the sounds, but merely ascertained if we both could hear something. I know what I had heard, but wanted Vince to confirm that he had experienced the same sounds before I would elaborate. Incidentally, if I had heard nothing, I would have made it evident. I always encourage team members to speak openly during investigations, rather than keeping quiet for fear of upsetting or contradicting other team members. This is one of the reasons why it is always beneficial to investigate in groups of no fewer than two if you split your team.

The sounds certainly seemed to have a 'distant' quality about them – they were kind of muffled, but they were definitely there. The castle has no other buildings around it so we can also rule out the noises coming from a neighbouring property.

3. Who or what was making the noises on the stairs in the King's Bedchamber?

I suppose it would be easy to say that Nick, who was possibly still half asleep, imagined these noises. However, he had actually been awake for some time before he heard them. In fact, when he was questioned he revealed that he had been awake for approximately 10 minutes, as he had looked at his watch when he woke up. He gauged that the sounds started a good few moments after he awoke; again he had checked his watch upon hearing the noises. What is unfortunate is that he thought the noises had been caused by either me or Stuart and so felt it unnecessary to check on them. I do believe that Nick heard something – but what that something was I'm not sure.

There have been reports of a Cavalier-like figure seen within the King's Bedchamber, as well as incidents of visitors being touched while in the room. Could these incidents be connected to the noises that were heard by Nick? Or could there be some other explanation?

I think the sticking point here is the fact that nothing was heard from those who were actually in the room, which is odd as I'm a very light sleeper, particularly when I am in unfamiliar surroundings.

THE EDINBURGH VAULTS, SCOTLAND, SECOND INVESTIGATION, 2005
EMF reading: 0
Outside temperature: 8°C
Inside temperature: 13°C
Weather conditions: Cold and raining with a slight breeze
Start time: 12.40 am

My second visit to Scotland's infamous Edinburgh Vaults was eagerly anticipated and had me wondering whether this investigation would be as fruitful as the first (see pages 59–63). Would the dreaded 'Mr Boots' put in an appearance tonight? Or would the cheeky little boy nicknamed Jack make his presence felt? I was again joined by Nick Scrimshaw and several guest investigators.

The investigation equipment for this particular visit to the Edinburgh Vaults was as follows:

- 2 digital video cameras with night-vision and tripods
- 1 EMF meter
- 1 infra-red thermometer (hand-held)
- 2 digital voice recorders
- 3 digital thermometers
- 2 trigger objects
- 2 digital still cameras
- 1 motion detector

Digital thermometers were positioned at various areas throughout the vaults and were periodically checked and noted, particularly the minimum/maximum readings. Digital still cameras were also used extensively during the entire investigation. Before starting we were given a tour of the location by our generous host for the night, Gary.

It wasn't too long before something strange occurred. While Gary was explaining a little about the history of the Edinburgh Vaults – keeping information pertaining to the

hauntings to a bare minimum in order to avoid the pitfalls of auto-suggestion or influencing the experiences of the investigators – I quite clearly heard a very peculiar noise. The best way I can describe it, is that it sounded like a metal dog tag rattling on a collar. What was even more exciting was that I was not the only one who heard the noise. As I looked around the area inquisitively, I noticed one of the other investigators doing exactly the same. I asked them if they had heard something, to which they confirmed that they had. It quickly became clear that we had both heard the same sound. This seemed like a good start to proceedings.

At about 1.10 am the first set of vigils began. The team was divided into two smaller groups. I took a team and headed to my chosen vigil area – the left-hand side of the vaults; the other group, led by Nick, took the right-hand side of the vaults.

This first set of vigils lacked activity, although a few orbs were captured on digital cameras within the main vault. Perhaps the evening wasn't going to be as exciting as promised after all. After 45 minutes or so, a brief break was called. At about 2.15 am our second set of vigils began, with the teams swapping locations.

At some point during this vigil I found myself in the Wine Cellar, along with our host Gary and two other invest-igators. It was while I was in this area that the first major incident took place. I was sitting on the edge of one of the area's alcoves talking quietly to the others about the ghost of the little boy named Jack when one of the investigators, who was sitting a few feet in front of me, suddenly shot to her feet and barged straight into me, knocking me further into the alcove. After a few frantic moments, which seemed to last an age, things calmed down and I was then able to determine what had just taken place.

Much shaken and visibly nervous, the young woman proceeded to explain that as she had been sitting on the floor she had suddenly felt a strong and definite tug on the back of her jeans, the result of which saw me unceremoniously bundled into the alcove in which I had been positioned.

OPPOSITE: *One of the haunted vaults at Edinburgh. Who or what put in an appearance during this investigation?*

ABOVE: *Nick Scrimshaw in action at the Edinburgh Vaults. The light trail is caused by Nick's torch beam, which was moving when this shot was taken.*

THIS EQUIPMENT WAS USED AS FOLLOWS:

- The digital video cameras were hand-held.
- The EMF meter was hand-held.
- One digital voice recorder was positioned in the main vault.
- The other digital voice recorder was positioned in the corridor at the rear of the vaults.
- One trigger object was set up on paper and positioned in the corridor at the rear of the vaults.
- The other trigger object was set up on paper and positioned in the area known as the Wine Cellar.
- The motion detector was positioned at various points throughout the investigation.

Ten minutes later another break was announced for refreshments and to enable us to discuss any experiences people may have encountered. Trigger objects were also checked for movement, but none could be detected. The motion detector was moved to a new position and the batteries changed.

A Strange Strangulation

After approximatley half an hour we began another vigil in the same area as we had done before, hoping for a continuation of earlier events. After a period of 50 minutes still nothing had happened, so I decided to shift areas and moved into the vault known as 'Mr Boot's room'. It was in this very location that our host, Gary, had undergone an exceptionally nasty experience on a previous occasion.

While he was hosting a tour one time, he had started to feel rather uncomfortable and then began to experience a choking sensation. Nevertheless he struggled on and continued with the event. Towards the end of the tour somebody approached him with some very strange news – his child had become increasingly agitated during that part of the tour, as he had seen a large man standing behind Gary, with his arms slowly wrapping around the tour guide's throat! As a result of this incident Mr Boot's room is not a favourite of Gary's – something that is completely understandable.

Anyway, I'd been sitting in the room for approximately 10 minutes talking to one of the investigating team members when they suddenly stopped mid-sentence. A worried look began to creep across her face. It appears that something – or possibly someone – had touched her on the arm. Nobody else was anywhere near her at the time.

The rest of the investigation passed without incident and before long I was homeward bound once again, ready to analyse the video footage and digital audio from the voice recorders. Apart from the odd faint noise that remains unexplained, nothing out of the ordinary was found on the audio or video footage. However, this trip to the Edinburgh Vaults raised several obvious questions.

LEFT: *The eerily atmospheric corridor that is located at the rear of the Edinburgh Vaults, links the two sides of the vault together.*

1. What was responsible, if anything, for tugging at the jeans of one of the investigators?
I suppose the easiest explanation would be to say that she imagined the whole incident. However, I have found that the imagination is not normally responsible for actual physical sensations or interaction in these circumstances, but instead tends to relate to sight and sound. It seems it is much easier to imagine that you've seen or heard something rather than actually felt something.

Suppose we cannot simply blame the imagination – what then was the cause? One thing is for certain, the experience, for this particular individual at least, was definitely real and on a physical level. It is worth noting that the little boy 'Jack' is apparently fond of tugging away at clothes, especially in this specific area within the Edinburgh Vaults.

2. What touched the team member in Mr Boot's room?
Well, you can realistically apply the same answer to the one above.

3. What was the noise heard by me and another team member at the start of the investigation?
The fact that two different people heard the same sound would seem to rule out imagination in this instance, and confirm that the noise did indeed exist (unless one of us had projected the thought telepathically – something that is highly doubtful).

However, it is much more difficult to establish exactly what the sound was. The noise seemed to emanate from a passage that was immediately to the right of where I was standing. There was nobody in that area at the time, as we were all standing together at that precise moment. In my initial description of the noise I had mentioned that it sounded similar to the rattle of a metal tag, like the kind that can be found on dog collars. This is more interesting than it would first appear, because one of the ghosts that has been witnessed in the vaults is that of a scruffy little dog!

Could it be that the sound we heard was the sound of a dog tag after all? Possibly. Personallly, however, I don't think the evidence based on hearing the noise just once throughout the entire investigation is solid enough to give a definite yes.

9

Other Paranormal Experiences

I'm fairly certain that nearly every one of you who happens to pick up this publication will know at least one person who will claim to have had a paranormal experience at some point or other during their life.

It seems that ghosts or spirits – call them what you will – have a habit of bumping into a fair few of us mere mortals. From phantom military personnel to ghostly animals, from children to aircraft, even, the list of these such encounters seems nigh on endless.

In this section you will hear from numerous individuals – some whom I know and others I do not – who have some pretty strange and thought-provoking experiences to share with us!.

And so, if you're sitting comfortably we shall begin. Read on...

Steven Nettleship and the Haunted Airbase Incident

Before we delve into this section, I thought I would share the story that gave me the idea for the chapter. I had been investigating some supposedly haunted locations, including an abandoned location called Nocton Hall, which had been used as an RAF hospital from the Second World War until it closed in 1983, and a rundown, disused airbase and barracks just two minutes walk away, which had also been used during the war. Many military sites seem to be haunted by ghosts, which range from crewmen to phantom aircraft. It's no surprise really when you consider just how much emotional stress such personnel must have experienced, especially in times of conflict. Could these incidents bolster the case for residual hauntings (see page 14)?

Along with my fellow investigators, I walked around these two locations eagerly, keeping a look-out for anything strange or paranormal in nature, but unfortunately nothing happened.

I then remembered that Steven Nettleship, a close friend of mine, had told me about an encounter he had once had at a disused airfield close to the village of Wymeswold, which could have been a residual haunting. The incident happened back in the late summer of 1994, when Steve was a Civilian Instructor teaching the air cadets from the Air Training Corps 209 Squadron (Nottingham). I contacted him to clarify the exact events. I have detailed his experience on the opposite page, so you can make up your own minds about what he encountered on that blustery night.

Of course, many other experiences similar to Steve's have been reported over the years, and not just at airfields. There are numerous reported incidents of ghostly figures roaming the sites where historic battles took place, such as Marston Moor, England or Culloden, Scotland, both of which saw violent and bloody fighting.

One final thing to address about haunted airfields involves those incidents that involve phantom aircraft. How can the ghost of an aircraft or any other inanimate object be seen? Well it seems to fall rather neatly into the concept of residual hauntings and the stone tape theory (see page 14).

Having remembered Steve's story, I set about finding other people with strange experiences to recount, which didn't prove too difficult, as there are thousands out there! So the rest of this section contains experiences I have collated from many individuals. These stories are the accounts of incidents that actually happened to the individuals involved or that were recounted to them by someone they trusted implicitly.

The purpose of these stories is to give you some idea of just how many people from different backgrounds have experienced events that they believe to be paranormal in origin.

STEVEN NETTLESHIP'S ACCOUNT: Occasionally during my time as a civilian instructor for the Air Training Corps the job would involve taking the cadets to (usually abandoned) airfields, and this day was one of those occasions.

The location consisted of approximately four buildings, all by the edge of a runway, most of which were in a rather ruinous condition, with the exception of the control tower.

Having just mentioned that the control tower was the only building not in a ruinous state, I have to briefly describe its condition for the sake of the story. The control tower was a two-storey-high building with a rooftop vantage/observation point. All the windows were missing, but the building itself was in a fair condition. To try and stop the tower getting any colder than was necessary from the windy conditions outside, I and the rest of the instructors positioned blue plastic sheeting over the window frames. This was also to provide a little bit of privacy for those of us who were going to sleep there after the exercises of the day were completed, myself included. The rest of the cadets were stationed outside using tents as their shelter, leaving the ground floor of the control tower for catering purposes and the first floor for the Civilian Instructors.

As the exercises drew to a close, we retired to our respective sleeping areas in preparation for the events to come the next day. By about 2am the wind had picked up and was now making the plastic sheeting flap against the window frames, making it difficult for anyone who was a light sleeper to stay asleep.

It was then that there was a loud bang, like a door being slammed shut. Having been virtually awake due to my restlessness, I rolled over in my sleeping bag to see where the noise had come from. I was now facing the control tower windows. I believe I had been awake for about five minutes when suddenly I became aware of a figure standing at the windows, a figure that at first I thought was another instructor who, like me, was unable to sleep.

As I stared at the figure by the window it dawned on me that something was not quite right. As my eyes had now become accustomed to looking at something in the dark, I could quite clearly make out that the figure was that of a man wearing a peaked cap and wearing some kind of US military uniform. Stranger still was the fact that this figure seemed to have his hands to his face as if looking through a pair of binoculars, and was looking out of the control tower windows... the same windows that had been totally covered by the blue plastic sheeting earlier on.

Thinking that I might just have mistaken one of the other instructors for the figure, I glanced over my shoulder to the other side of the room where the rest of the team were sleeping. Everybody was asleep.

Again I turned my gaze back towards the figure at the windows and was startled at what I saw – nothing!. In the space of what amounted to less than 10 seconds, the figure that I had seen looking out of the windows had vanished without a trace. It goes without saying that the remainder of my sleep was even more uncomfortable than before.

In the morning I decided that I had to put my mind at rest and find some kind of logical explanation for what I had witnessed, so I quizzed the rest of the Civilian Instructors and even the cadets (who, if you remember, had been sleeping outside).

I asked them who had been awake at around 2 am and at the control tower windows, but the answers I received confirmed what I suspected – that nobody from the group was responsible. To this day I still do not know who the figure was and what it was looking for out of the control tower windows.

Richard Jones, Rait Castle, Near Nairn, Scotland

This story was supplied by my good friend, the author, historian and paranormal enthusiast Richard Jones.

Richard has spent years scouring the length and breadth of Britain in search of stories concerning ghosts, hauntings and the paranormal. And, when he isn't doing that, you can often find him hosting his world-famous City of London Ghost Walks and Jack the Ripper Walks.

I have long been an admirer of Richard's books and have numerous titles he has written. Someone who is very much used to visiting this kind of location, Richard does not scare that easily, something I can certainly vouch for, having worked with him on a number of different occasions.

RICHARD JONES' ACCOUNT: Rait Castle is one of the creepiest locations I have ever visited. It skulks in brooding desolation, surrounded by dark woodlands, and can be a sinister place even on a bright summer's day, as I discovered when I visited it while on a research trip.

To get to the castle you have to trudge across a number of muddy fields. You then enter an area of woodland, on the edge of which the ruined castle stands.

When I went to the castle, having entered the ruined interior, I heard the distinct sound of footsteps walking around inside. I went to [investigate] where I thought they had come from, but found nothing. Suddenly, despite the fact it was 10 am on a bright August morning, the temperature began to drop alarmingly and I was overcome with the most dreadful feeling of foreboding I have ever experienced. I don't normally scare that easily, but I couldn't get out of the place fast enough.

To this day I cannot explain what happened or prove whether it was anything paranormal. But this was one of the few occasions in my life when I have experienced abject fear for something unknown.

Sarah Hall – Strange Phenomena At Lumley Castle Hotel

Some of the best locations in which to hold paranormal investigations appear to be hotels. One can imagine how many people pass through their doors and spend time within the rooms – some may even return now and again in spectral form! Britain has more than its fair share of very old and supposedly haunted properties that have been converted into hotels and it is thought that renovations to such buildings can stir up an increase in paranormal phenomena.

In the following case, I find it very interesting to hear that nothing had actually been moved, although the furniture movement caused quite a lot of noise. It would appear that what the witnesses actually experienced was an audio-only replay of events that may have happened in the past in that room, which is a very common phenomenon at haunted locations. But it would also seem that this particular hotel is the dwelling place for a poltergeist, judging by the way that Sarah described the tray being wedged in the table legs and the mysteriously moving cigarette that flew off the table.

The noise of the furniture being moved about would not be attributed to a poltergeist. As mentioned earlier in this book and ascertained by the numerous poltergeist case reports (see Chapter 2, pages 20–23), poltergeist activity is much more physical in nature and in some cases becomes violent. Furniture and other objects are much more likely to actually move if a poltergeist is present, you wouldn't just hear the sounds of the movement.

SARAH HALL'S ACCOUNT: At the time of these events I was working at Lumley Castle Hotel, where I had worked for about 12 years, mainly behind the bars. The hotel has a number of different function rooms, including the Northumbria Room on the top floor and the Scarborough Room directly beneath. The Northumbria Room did not have a bar, and so we had to set one up in the snooker room next door. This involved moving a lot of stuff around, and so we always placed a chair close by the bar, so that we could rest during the shift. We always put the chair opposite the door, which looked out to a small lobby area, then out to the third-floor landing, and onto a fake wall with an arch through which you could enter the residents' areas of the hotel. This meant that we could see if anyone was coming – particularly the management!

One night things were moving very slowly. We were hosting an 80th birthday party for about 14 people, a few of whom were drinking. So I helped the waiting staff when I could and also sat in the chair looking across the landing, hoping that the dull night would pass swiftly.

Suddenly I noticed what appeared to be a woman's head and shoulders reflected in the mirror at the far end of the landing. The glass was attached to a bureau, and was very old. It had lost some of its silver backing, and so often looked odd depending on the light. I told a few other staff members and they could all see the figure. One approached it, and said it just disappeared, as if a switch had been flicked off. He also said there was no erosion of the background as there was in some other parts of the mirror. This made us all very uneasy, and was not the only time this area gave us something to talk about.

One night the Function Manager, Duty Manager, a security guard and myself were sitting in the Scarborough Room having a break. We chatted for a while, when the Function Manager pointed out that whoever was setting up the Northumbria Room was being so rough that there would barely be any furniture left.

The Duty Manager checked his notes and said that the room was already set up as the keys had been handed back in. The porter in charge of the Northumbria Room had left about an hour earlier. The two rooms were not just accessible by the main stairs, but also by a secret set of spiral stairs, which were certainly not well known – some of the staff didn't even know they were there! We all ran to place ourselves at points from where the person in the room would be seen as they left the room. The Duty Manager was concerned about the equipment in there, including laptop computers, which were ready for the meeting the next day. The Function Manager, whose name was Keith, had a key and tried to let himself into the Northumbria Room. As he unlocked the door, he felt it being pushed roughly from the other side. Keith pushed back and the door opened just enough for him to thrust a camera into the room and take pictures – a habit forced on him by me! The door pushed shut again and he shouted out in alarm. The other guys became scared and ran back down the spiral stairs.

I had stayed at the bottom. No one could have gone up the stairs, as the rooms up there were not habitable – some had floors missing – and no one passed me on the way back down. The pictures taken by the Function Manager showed a few orbs, which are not events I deem to be paranormal. What was interesting, however, is that despite the extensive dragging of furniture, banging and clattering about, not a single piece of furniture had actually been moved. Even if someone was joking, there would have been evidence of movement. Interestingly, on entering this room in the past, guests had noted that Lumley Castle headed-notepaper had been written on – yet a porter always sets up a clean room and it is checked by two managers before being locked up.

The woman whose face we saw in the mirror was also seen in the Scarborough Room. On another occasion, while three of us were having a break, I noticed the reflection of another person sitting with us through the window at the far end of the room. I said nothing in the hope someone else would see her. One of the waitresses did notice the woman and she was so scared she would not come back into the room. Keith, who was with us during this incident, is sensitive to these things, and often knew before all of us if someone was there. He asked me if I could see her in the window. Given that he had his back to the window at the time, I was surprised by his comment, as you can probably imagine.

Once Keith was touched on the shoulder in this room. He was talking to one of the bar staff and I was standing to one side of him. We all heard and felt the floor move, but the whole room was visible, we didn't even think about it – that is until we saw Keith turn, as though someone was behind him. He jumped, shouted and then turned white. He said someone had just tapped him on the shoulder. But there was no one else in the room.

Another room at the hotel in which strange phenomena have been experienced is the Baron's Bar, which serves as the bar for the Baron's Hall. One night, while we were tidying the bar before the next set of guests came in, I noticed that one of the tables had a tray on it. I made a mental note to go back and get it, but when I did it had gone, so I assumed someone else had moved it. I turned around to find that it had been shoved between the four legs of another table; the tables were small and round, with four legs joined together by wooden posts. It would take some effort to get a round object inside a square object of roughly the same size!

I turned back to where the tray had been, to see a cigarette, which I had not noticed earlier. I asked my colleagues who had moved the tray and a horrified look swept across their faces as they watched what happened next. With no draught in the room, nobody walking by and no other external force, the cigarette shot off the table as if it has been flicked away.

We were never able to reproduce the movement without using our hands – no vibration or draught moved the cigarette, nor did it move in the same way if the table was knocked.

Chris Thomas – The Godolphin Hotel Incident

This next incident came to me from a member of a paranormal investigation group know as the Believe Team, which is based in Lincolnshire. They are one of the youngest paranormal investigation groups I have worked with.

Chris Thomas is a teenager, but has had a keen interest in the paranormal world for a number of years and he approaches such matters with a healthy degree of rationality and scepticism.

The incident outlined opposite took place a few years ago, but it left an impact on Chris that is still with him to this day.

Judging from what happened to him that night, it would appear that he experienced poltergeist activity of some kind.

It is interesting to note that Chris also witnessed a drop in temperature moments before the incident with the scissors, something that numerous witnesses of supposed paranormal activity experience. Also of note is the fact that he had no idea about the ghostly woman who haunts the kitchen. Indeed, he had no real interest in things of a paranormal nature at that point. We can presume from the way he described the scissors flying across the room that they did not simply drop off the hook on which they were hanging. Finally, I think it is also very interesting to consider the fact that Chris was drinking in the kitchen, as this activity appears to relate to the story of the woman who is known to haunt this particular spot and her apparent dislike for it. Perhaps, she was showing her displeasure by throwing the scissors across the kitchen – which is a little bit harsh, if you ask me!

Since this incident, Chris has formed an investigation group, has conducted numerous over-nighters and has even been approached by several broadcast companies – all of whom are intererested in his paranormal exploits!

Anyway, here is his story...

CHRIS THOMAS' ACCOUNT: While I lived in Cornwall, I worked at a hotel called the Godolphin, which was situated in the seaside town of Newquay. I was about 15 years old and had just been to a skate park, so I was rather tired at the time. I had been working in this hotel for around six months and had no idea about any hauntings or ghost stories associated with the place. To some, it was a spooky old building, but to me it was just a hotel. On July 20th I was called in early, as one of the staff members called in sick. It was a very busy day, and when I finished my shift at about 9 pm I was offered refreshments, so I sat down near the kitchen and chilled out for a while. Suddenly, I could hear cooking pans knocking against each other nearby. I went to check it out, but as I started walking towards the area the noise stopped. I sat back down, not really thinking

much of it, when suddenly the room became icy cold. It got so cold that I could see my breath in front of me, and condensation began to form on the windows next to me. At this point I became a little concerned as to why it had become so cold, so I decided to make sure that the back door wasn't open. As soon as I got off my chair the taps turned on next to me, and I witnessed a pair of scissors fly off a hook and travel straight across the room. What was strange was that I didn't find it scary at the time and I didn't consider that it could be some sort of paranormal activity. When I went to pick up the scissors they were very cold for some

reason and that intrigued me. I put them back on the hook and went home thinking nothing of the experience. The next day I came back into work, and found that a customer had reported something making loud banging noises in the kitchen last night, which was rather strange as I'd locked the room so there couldn't have been anyone in there. I then asked the manager if she had ever witnessed any paranormal phenomena in the building. She replied that an old lady haunts the kitchen, which used to be the lounge. She apparently hates people drinking in this area. What had I been doing when I'd had the experience? I'd been drinking some cola! Now I still remain a sceptic, but I do have to admit that I am baffled as to what could make a pair of scissors fly across a room. And to find out the next day that the ghost of a lady roams around the kitchen area was extremely interesting. Did my experience link with previous hauntings at the Godolphin Hotel?

Before this incident, I didn't really have any interest in ghosts or anything to do with the unexplained. I had never experienced anything in my life that could be seen as paranormal activity. After the experience I became a lot more interested in the paranormal. I am sceptical about such matters, but I still have no rational explanation for what did occur that night. I have never conducted a séance or a ouija board session, as I believe you can obtain more tangible evidence if you don't have any physical contact with such experiments.

Kevin Ling – An Encounter With A Suicide Victim?

As you would expect, any building that was used in times of crisis or war would have been very highly charged with emotions emanating from the people associated with the location at the time. Britain has numerous military bases and buildings that saw action in the 20th century's two world wars. Some of these buildings are still used, but others have been abandoned. They often seem to be frequented by ghostly figures, many of which used to actually work at the base in question. With so many of these bases and buildings still in active use today, it probably comes as little surprise to hear that sightings of phantom military personnel are among the most commonly reported paranormal phenomena. In fact, several people who were investigating one such RAF airbase with me in Lincolnshire witnessed what they believed to be a military figure running into the designated crew-room for the night. It was established afterwards that nobody had entered the room, which had housed at least three people at the time, and there was no way this figure could have left the area unless it had run past the investigating team members again, which it didn't.

In addition to the account opposite, Kevin also supplied two more tales, one involving his father and another relating to his local pub and its landlord (see the following pages). Although they are not first-hand accounts they are still interesting.

Q & A: KEVIN LING

I asked people who supplied their personal stories five questions, designed to give me more of an insight into their history, and their paranormal experience. Here's what Kevin said:

How old were you when the apparent paranormal experience occurred and where were you?
I was 18. The incident took place at Crowborough Army Camp, East Sussex.

Were you (to the best of your knowledge) going through any stressful, emotional or psychological events at the time of the incident?
I can't recall being particularly stressed [or emotional] ... just the normal teenage angst and concern about who was going to buy me my next pint!

Did you believe in the paranormal, ghosts and hauntings prior to the incident?
I was a believer before that incident.

And after the experience, what are your beliefs?
I remain a firm believer in the paranormal, though it is only in recent years that I've really started to further my interest and find out more about it.

Have you ever taken part in a séance or ouija board session?
Up to then, I'd never taken part in any ouija board session or séance, only recently did I partake in a séance at about 5 am at Battle Abbey, Hastings – [I was] almost asleep at the time – needless to say nothing happened! I have had quite a bit more success with glass divination at various locations and though I'm quite convinced personally I appreciate that most others have yet to be so.

KEVIN LING'S FIRST ACCOUNT: I have an incident that I, as believer who is easily convinced, would consider paranormal. It took place in the summer of 1981 when I was a fresh-faced youth of 18. I was working for the Property Services Agency at the time and as part of my training I worked at Crowborough Army camp in East Sussex. At the time the base was used for training cadets, with occasional visits from regular soldiers who were on exercises there. My duties included carrying out condition surveys, which involved making notes about the condition of a building. I had to do this for all the buildings on this site to see what general maintenance was required.

Anyway, the incident in question occurred when I was carrying out a survey in the NAAFI building, which was a collection of serving areas, bars and dining areas, with more rooms to the rear, all of which led off each other. The building was huge. Even back then I held a keen interest in ghosts and the paranormal and if I am honest I was already aware that the building was supposed to be haunted, but I didn't know by what or whom.

It was midsummer and a blisteringly hot day, with little or no air movement. It was very warm inside the building and many of the windows were being replaced so through-out the building there were large holes in the external walls, which would obviously serve as a source for draughts, although as I've said there was no wind and everywhere was uncomfortably warm.

The incident occurred in a long room, which I imagine in years gone by would have been some sort of ballroom. I'll admit that I was on edge, knowing the place was supposed to be haunted – it was so big and there weren't many people around, so it was eerily quiet. It wasn't a sighting, but a cold feeling that I experienced, as I slowly moved towards the corner of the room by a set of double doors. (I'd entered by another set of double doors located at the other end of the room).

Suddenly the temperature seemed to plummet – it was literally freezing for a period of 10 seconds or so, but as I passed the door things seemed to return to normal. I didn't associate this with anything paranormal at the time, although I did wonder where the breeze could have come from, as I was at the point in the room that was furthest from any open window.

I finished what I was doing and went to see the NAAFI Manageress to tell her I had done. She made me a cup of tea and not wanting to miss an opportunity I urged her to tell me the story of the ghost. Apparently several things had been seen and heard, including black figures that were spotted darting across corridors and the sounds of furniture being thrown about behind closed shutters, which revealed no apparent movement of these objects when opened.

However it was the final thing she told me that set me thinking. She referred to the room I had been in and told me that it had been used as a temporary morgue during the Second World War. A young nurse who used to work there had apparently hanged herself in the corner of the room one day, after discovering that the latest body to be wheeled in was that of her fiancé. Since that time, many people have reported a sudden drop in temperature in that very corner – it was, of course, the same one that I had been standing in. I didn't bother to mention my alleged experience to her, not wanting her to think I was just saying it for effect. I felt quite touched, if not a little sad, about the story and as you will probably gather have never forgotten it. I often wonder if it was just my imagination (although I wasn't aware of that particular story beforehand), or whether it was truly paranormal.

I haven't been back to the site since, so couldn't tell you if anything further has happened, although I often drive past the entrance and wonder whether anything has happened.

Kevin Ling – The Phantom Highwayman and the Ghostly Pub

As far as this second report from Kevin – of a highwayman experience – goes, it is a regularly reported incident along many of Britain's roads and country lanes. The fact that this was a multiple witness account adds substance to the sighting.

One individual who has been seen on numerous occasions is perhaps *the* most famous highwayman of them all – Dick Turpin. For those who do not know, Turpin was a highwayman, murderer and horse thief who plied his trade in the 18th century in and around Essex and London. He eventually fled his hideout in Epping Forest after accidentally killing his companion Tom King, who had just been captured by the local constabulary – Turpin was actually aiming for the policemen holding King at the time. Before he died, Turpin's accomplice managed to provide the authorities with vital information about the highwayman, so Turpin set off for Yorkshire where he made a base from which he frequently made journeys into the nearby county of Lincolnshire to steal sheep and horses. He eventually felt the hangman's noose in 1739.

Britain has countless haunted pubs and watering holes. In fact, nearly every old pub or coaching inn in which you might find yourself can probably boast of having at least one ghostly inhabitant lurking within, and it would appear that many of them are actually former customers! Check out your local and you may be surprised to learn that it too has a spectral customer or even former resident or two hanging around!

KEVIN LING'S OTHER ACCOUNTS: My father and two of his friends were travelling to Plymouth in a Mini when a figure that could only be described as a highwayman stepped out in front of them. Unable to stop they ran straight over him and thinking they'd finished off some drunk from a fancy dress party, they screeched to a halt and set out to find him, but, as you can probably guess, there was nobody to be seen! As reality dawned all you could hear was the banging of three doors as my father and his friends scrambled back inside the car – although he believes they ran out of petrol about 30 miles outside of town, their wheels never touched the ground.

The other story I have involves my local pub, the Wishing Tree in Hollington, and though I've never seen anything there for myself, a number of incidents have been reported in recent times. While chatting with the landlord on New Year's Eve we counted at least seven occasions on which people claimed to have seen or felt things within the previous 18 months. These incidents included a toilet flushing on its own in the ladies' toilet while the landlord's son-in-law was cleaning. In the same toilet a girl reported an incident during which she didn't shut the cubicle door fully; she saw a figure walk towards the window and glance in at her, she apologized at her lack of dignity, but when she came out there was nobody else in the room – even though nobody had walked back past the door and there was nowhere else for the figure to go. On another occasion the landlady felt something push past her through the opening from the saloon to the public bar, while somebody sitting at the end of public bar reported seeing the silhouette or outline of a woman's figure walking out into the bar. Another incident occurred on the upper floor, when a cleaning lady turned to see a woman dressed in black standing on the stairs and looking at her. She said good morning to her, but the figure slowly vanished. The landlord also recalled how he once rose for work at 6 am to hear the sound of a dog barking and a voice telling it to shut up. He was pretty sure the sounds came from outside, but almost immediately afterwards he heard the voice of a little girl softly saying 'Mummy, Mummy', which he was convinced was in the same room. Looking through the windows at the front and back of the building, it was clear that there was nobody to be seen. Thinking that either his wife or young son might have been responsible for the noise he went to check, but they were both sound asleep elsewhere in the building. The previous landlord reported how one night, having switched off the lights and gone upstairs, he looked through an upstairs window and through a lower window into the bar, only to see that the light to the shove-ha'penny board – which he was convinced he turned off – was back on. Thinking someone was downstairs he returned with the family dog. As they returned to the bar, the dog's hackles rose and he started to bark. The landlord approached the light to switch it off again, and the area around it went icy cold.

Another incident in the pub involved the current landlord's three-year-old grandson. He toddled into the public bar lavatories, only to come straight back out and ask his mother if she could get the lady to move because he wanted to go to the toilet. She and her boyfriend returned to the toilet with the child, but although he could apparently see the lady and pointed towards her, they saw and felt nothing.

Other events have involved items such as coffee mugs and paperwork moving, only to reappear in the same place later on and lights coming on by themselves, despite the switches being behind locked doors. Several other people have experienced strange things in the pub, many of whom are reluctant to talk about their experiences, primarily because they fear the subsequent mocking. This makes me feel that there is definitely something going on in the pub.

Riad Thomas – A Murdered Family Returns

Kevin Ling put me in touch with Riad Thomas, who also had an interesting tale to tell. Many a paranormal enthusiast would be envious at the activity and sightings that he experienced when he was younger...

I'm sure you will all agree that the following set of incidents is fascinating, to say the least. It is not uncommon to hear of stories in which young children have been known to 'see' ghosts; a bit like the character in the film *The Sixth Sense*. Some people actually theorize that this is because children are not occupied with the same stresses, worries and pressures that adults contend with every day. So perhaps it is the case that children have a more relaxed and open-minded mental state, perfect for 'tuning in' to the spirit realm.

As I have mentioned previously in this very book, there are numerous parts of the brain that science cannot yet fathom. Could it be that some people have an area of the brain that allows them to 'see' into a ghostly realm? Who can say?

As Riad eventually found out, it is always worth trying to uncover the history of a location that seems to be haunted, as this may help to figure out why spirits are present in the first place and give you some insight into how to put an end to the incidents if necessary.

Some people reading this may think that the events that surrounded Riad could simply be put down to an overactive imagination. However, it is worth remembering that Riad's sister witnessed the 'big man' standing in the doorway *at the same time* as her brother. And so, unless one or both of them is telepathic, which I doubt, this would seem to indicate that there was *something* in the room that they were both able to see, and from different viewpoints too.

The stone tape and residual haunting theories (see page 14) could also be applied in this case, as an emotionally charged event had taken place in the very room in which the paranormal phenomena was occurring. Had the very materials used in the fabrication of the house somehow absorbed the energy from these events and played them back under a certain set of conditions in a similar way to a cinematic projection? Or had Riad's mental condition, being young and perhaps more open-minded, somehow allowed him to access the latent energy that had built up in the room many years previously?

This is a definite possibility, but it would not provide an explanation as to why Riad saw his dog as a ghostly form days *before* his pet had passed away in a road accident. Again, this is all theoretical so please make up your own minds about the case.

RIAD THOMAS' ACCOUNT: My experiences began shortly after my father died in 1976, when I was five years old. At that time, we were living in a detached house in the Hastings area.

I can clearly recall evenings when my sister and I would hear my mother screaming downstairs and and we would head down towards her to find rows of books on the floor and, in one case, a window that had been broken from the outside. My mother, who believed in spiritual matters, told us we had poltergeists.

My very first sighting was on a Saturday morning, as we were waiting in the lounge for a taxi to take us to the supermarket. I looked into the hall and saw what appeared to be a pair of legs in white tights run along the hall and up the stairs. I was adamant that I had seen them. My mother, I think wishing to prove me wrong, went upstairs to look. When she returned she was quite pale – it turned out that despite having shut and checked all the first floor windows earlier, her bedroom window was wide open. Furthermore, the daffodils at ground level outside the window were trampled. We moved house shortly after that.

The next house we moved to was a big, old semi-detached that overlooked a park. We spent ages redecorating the place, stripping away timber panelling and floors. At the back of the house was an annexe with a bedroom, which my mum used. In the summer of 1978 we took on students and opened the house as a bed and breakfast. That summer we had one student who was always good fun and used to pass the time with my sister and me. I remember waking up one night and feeling very cold; no windows were open despite the hot summer.

I turned over and by the door of my room was a very tall figure with what looked like a white sheet over his head. His hands were held up in the air above him and, although I could not see him, I could see his black eyes. I sensed his mouth was open in a snarl rather than ready for conversation.

I still shiver when I recall trying to shout for my mother, but my throat had dried in fear and I made no sound. I buried my face in the bed and did not look up. I must have fallen asleep as the next thing I knew it was morning, with the summer sun pouring in through the large windows. I told my mum, but she didn't believe it was a ghost; instead she thought it was the student playing a trick on me. I asked him, but he denied it, laughing.

My experience was put down to nothing more sinister than a a bad dream. However, that night exactly the same thing happened again. After four consecutive nights my mother suggested that I should see a doctor. Over that weekend nothing happened, and as we were due to go on holiday, the whole thing was forgotten.

Whilst we were on holiday my grandparents were staying in the house. My grandmother had always claimed that she experienced premonitions and told us a grey lady visited her, usually when something traumatic happened in the family. When my cousin died in a car crash in 1980, the grey lady visited my grandmother several days before and after the accident.

While we were on holiday my grandmother awoke every night and saw the grey lady at the foot of her bed. She was very concerned for our safe return. I later found out that I was due to see a psychiatrist when we returned from holiday, but my grandmother took my mother to one side and told her about her sightings of the grey lady – she felt that something bad was occurring in the house. My mum was not sure what to do, but decided to postpone my appointment with the psychiatrist.

Following our holiday I was given a copy of the Bible and a camera so that I could record anything untoward that happened in the bedroom... It did. Within just days of our return from holiday the big man was back, menacing me from the end of the bed. I had a little more confidence after my grandmother's experience and stared at him for a while, noticing that I could see both the light switch and the door through his white sheet. Eventually, I hid beneath the covers clutching my Bible. The next night I tried to take a photograph with very shaky hands – I do not know what happened to that film!

One night in September that year, I remember waking up, but without the feelings of cold and trepidation that came before the big man's previous visits. I sat up in bed and saw an old lady sitting in a rocking chair by the window. She stared across the room and rocked gently. She was not menacing in anyway, so I just stared at her from my pillow until I eventually fell asleep.

The next night the old woman was joined by a little boy, who looked exactly like me except for two things – his clothes were scruffy and torn and he floated six inches off the floor.

The following night the pair of them returned; only this time, our dog, Dougal, was sitting at the boy's feet. Each morning I would tell my mother what I had seen. She was not sure what to do, offering to move to my bedroom – something that, despite a lack of bravery, I was unwilling to accept. The following evening our dog was run over and eventually had to be put down by the vet.

That night I saw the old lady, the boy and dog once more.

It was then decided that my sister should join me in the same bedroom. On the very first night she joined me she woke me up. She sat straight up in her bed staring at

the door – the big man was back once again, and this time somebody else had seen him. We both tried to take photographs of the figure, but I think that our shaking hands, combined with utter fear, prevented us from doing anything more than huddling together. We told nobody what had happened in the room while we were still living at that house.

However, as time wore on my mother's fears grew stronger and stronger and she mentioned the strange occurrences to our neighbours.

Living next door to us at the time were three generations of the same family. The grandmother, who was then in her nineties, told us that she remembered something from her past that struck a chord. She had kept all of the local newspapers in their basement and a few weeks later she found the article that she had been thinking of. The headline read 'FAMILY MURDERED, HUSBAND KILLS HIMSELF' – on the cover of the faded newspaper was a picture of our house.

It transpired that during the 1930s a terrible tragedy had occured in our house to the members of the family that was living there at the time... A man had killed his wife, mother-in-law and son, and after murdering the three of them, he had then hanged himself. All the deaths had occurred in the front bedroom where I had been sleeping. This explained some of the activity I had experienced; the only mystery was that I had never once seen the ghost of the man's wife. My experiences ended later that year when a Brazilian student 'blessed' us, carrying out a ritual with candles and giving us special necklaces to wear for a year – her father was some kind of traditional doctor in Brazil.

Incidentally, these hauntings began shortly after my mother had had some friends over for an evening at the ouija board.

Abigail Quinn's Experiences

The following reports come from Abigail Quinn who lives in Aberdeen. Abigail is quite lucky, as she actually works in a reputedly haunted location – Leith Hall, and also lives in a haunted flat. This is beneficial in that she knows the building in which she works is haunted and is less likely to imagine any experiences as a result of simple over-excitement.

Leith Hall is a location I have investigated in the past and it has a very intriguing history. John Leith, who Abigail mentions in her report, was apparently murdered. He was shot in the head during a row in a tavern and was brought to the hall where he died some time later, or so the story goes. He has haunted Leith Hall ever since and his ghostly form has been seen in numerous parts of the property.

Were Abigail's experiences anything to do with him? Perhaps he was letting her know that she is a welcome addition to the tour staff by offering a reassuring hand on the shoulder. Or was there somebody else making themselves known in this fashion? And what about the experience in the Children's Room, where she saw the bright light and began to feel uncomfortable? Was there a more sinister presence trying to make her aware that they did not appreciate her company at that moment in time?

I would be interested to hear if Abigail does any research into her current abode and finds anything that may be relevant to what she has witnessed. Although the property is of a fair age, this alone does not guarantee that it is haunted; far too many people seem to automatically associate the age of a building with whether or not it will be haunted. I'm certain that many of you would attest to new buildings having just as much chance of being haunted as older ones.

Q & A: ABIGAIL QUINN

How old were you when the apparent paranormal experience occurred and where were you?
I was 33, in Aberdeen. Leith Hall and my flat.

Did you believe in the paranormal, ghosts and hauntings prior to the incident?
For many years I have believed in the paranormal in general; however, I would have to label myself a sceptical believer as I will not accept things on face value if there are other possible explanations that are of a more earthly nature.

And after the experience, what are your beliefs?
Since taking a more active stance to find proof that the paranormal and spirit world exists, I have had experiences that reassure me on a personal level, but I have also experienced many things that cause me to question what has previously been accepted as paranormal phenomena. The most interesting has been the psychological dynamics of group investigations where I have willingly sat back to watch the behaviour of the 'investigators' as much, if not more so, than the location and occurrences themselves. After all of my experiences, I still believe, but I think I've developed a more logical and rational approach to such experiences.

Have you ever taken part in a séance or ouija board session?
I have been involved in séances before, and have been involved in numerous ouija board sessions.

ABIGAIL QUINN'S FIRST ACCOUNT

Location: Leith Hall
When: Early Summer 2005
Weather: Dry, warm and sunny
Time: Mid-afternoon, Sunday

I was a new volunteer tour guide at Leith Hall and was still accompanying the existing guides on their tours. I had been volunteering for about two weeks. On one particular tour I took a group into the dining room, which is the first room at the top of the stairs on the first floor. I was standing with my back close to the wall to the right of the door, which I had closed once the group had entered the room. There was nobody within 2-3 feet of me and no one at all to my left. As I was listening to another tour guide a couple of minutes into this section of the tour, I suddenly became aware of a hand being placed on my left shoulder. I experienced all of the physical sensations involved, for example the heat of the hand, the length of the fingers and so on. It was a large hand and probably belonged to a male if I were to hazard a guess. It was not at all a menacing or negative feeling. It felt very much like a comforting action or, as my friend later suggested, a welcoming one. The whole event left me feeling very calm and happy and I remember ending this particular tour with a big smile on my face. The sensation lasted for approximately 10 seconds, although it felt like longer, and I did not move until the feeling disappeared. When the feeling did disappear, it was not a fading sensation; it felt exactly like someone taking his or her hand off my shoulder.

When the feeling went away, I immediately looked behind me to see whether I had been leaning against a picture frame, but there weren't any near me. I was also keen to see if there was a dado rail that I may have been leaning against, but there wasn't one in this room. The only other possibility was that the clothes I was wearing at the time caused the sensation, so for the next five or so minutes I played with my jumper and bra-strap to try to replicate the feeling! I must have looked very odd, it was lucky I was at the back of the group!

A few weeks later I also experienced a strong smell of sweet tobacco in the entrance hall of the building. It was a hot, summer Sunday afternoon and we had had no visitors for some time. As quickly as I sensed the odour, it disappeared; it didn't fade, although it was very apparent for at least 30 seconds to a minute or so.

ABIGAIL QUINN'S SECOND ACCOUNT

Location: Leith Hall
When: October 2005
Weather: Cold and damp but no rain
Time: Approximately 7 pm (dark)

Another event took place in the Children's Bedroom at Leith Hall on the Friday before Hallowe'en. I was due to take a group of adults around the house to tell them ghost stories before a ghost walk through the gardens. I planned to make the tales as realistic as possible. John Leith had died in the Children's Bedroom, so I was planning on telling his story while in there. About half an hour before the event, I decided to take a quick walk through the house by myself to note how long it would take to get the group through the route. I went straight through the corridor and into the music room where I rehearsed my lines. I then went into the Children's Bedroom to continue with John's story. At this time, the lights had all been dimmed in preparation for the tour and this bedroom was the darkest room of the whole house. The only light was in the Turret Room and there was a dark net draped in front of the half-glass panelled door. As a result, two thirds of the room was in almost total darkness. I stood near this door so that I could refer to my notes should I need them, but I faced the darkest corner of the room while speaking. As I entered the room I was aware of an uncomfortable atmosphere, my heart began to beat faster and I confess that I suddenly felt a little nervous. I have to state that while I am happy in all areas of the house, this is the one room that tends to have a different atmosphere.

It is also often a naturally very cold room, but on this occasion I began to feel very warm and the heat appeared to me to feel very oppressive. I began to talk quietly, repeating John's story. About halfway through the narrative a very bright flash of light illuminated the room. It wasn't a momentary flash, but was more like a bright lamp being switched on and then off again a second or two later. The core of the light source was approximately waist-height. I was also conscious of the air feeling electrified – it's hard to explain, but it was the feeling of static. I didn't leave the room immediately but actually stayed and asked if there was anyone with me. The general atmosphere in the room remained, but nothing else happened. I was very nervous by now and not unhappy to leave the room to continue my rehearsal. Walking into the next room made me very aware of the temperature difference, as this next room was noticeably cooler and I immediately felt calmer. A few minutes later, Linda, the Property Manager, came to find me. I told her what had happened and she was quite excited to hear about it. She added that early that same morning, at approximately 3 am, she had been woken by the intruder alarm in the house. Coincidentally, the only activation of the intruder alarm was in the Children's Bedroom. Apparently this has never happened before or since.

ABIGAIL QUINN'S THIRD ACCOUNT

Location: My flat
When: Ongoing
Time: Evening/night
Activity: Intermittent occurrences rather than continuous

I've lived in my flat in Torry, Aberdeen, for almost two years. It is about 106 years old. Ever since I moved in I have been aware of a presence that roams the flat and seems to emanate from what is now my kitchen. It is not unlikely that my kitchen was once the bedroom of the flat — some of the other flats are still laid out this way. When I moved in, what is now my bedroom did not have a bed or other furniture and I slept in the living room next to the kitchen for a few weeks. During this time, but only when it was dark, I was drawn to the doorway of the kitchen where there is a half-glass panelled door, which I always keep shut at night. I have no explanation why, but even now I am nervous of being in the living room when this door is open. The most interesting part of this story concerns the first time my friend came to visit, around May or June 2004. I had never mentioned anything about the feelings I had experienced at this time and I made up a bed in the living room for her. The next morning, she told me she had not slept well at all as she was very nervous about the kitchen doorway and said she kept expecting someone to walk out of there. To this day, she insists on having her bed made up in my bedroom and refuses to sleep in the living room!

One evening in March 2005 I was preparing to go to bed when I reached the living room light switch and was suddenly compelled to turn around to look across the room and into the kitchen. While I did not want to do this, I could not walk away without looking and before I switched off the light, I saw a person walk across the doorway from right to left. I stayed where I was for a few moments trying to rationalize what I saw and then retreated to my bedroom where my light stayed on for some time while I tried to figure out what I'd seen. I do have to state that at this time, I was still grieving over the sudden death of my lovely mother, who had passed away in January of that year.

Over the months since I moved in, I've felt the presence less and less, although I do tend to put the lights on when walking through the living room to the kitchen at night. One other occurrence of note is a funnel of cool air that springs up to the right of my bedroom fireplace; this is not used and has plasterboard covering it, as well as my bed being positioned in front of it. The funnel seems to reach from the floor to approximately 4– 5 feet upwards. Its width is approximately 1 foot across. This has happened on three occasions in differing weather conditions and on one occasion in the daytime, when my friend also experienced it.

While I have had many other experiences in the past, these are the most recent and consciously evaluated ones; events that, to me, have more credibility.

Anne McAviney — The Malevolent Monk

Spectral monks are among the most widely reported phenomena when it comes to actual sightings of ghosts and you'd be surprised at the number of locations they seem to pop up at, including buildings that appear not to have a connection to religion at all. We seem to forget that the present location of a property can sometimes occupy the site of a building that existed hundreds of years previously. Some of these ancient sites and foundations may well have a connection to a religious dwelling. I know of a number of locations that have been built upon the foundations of what was formerly an abbey, priory or monastery. In some of these properties you can actually still see the foundations of these historic buildings at cellar level and many are home to sightings of monks that are still being recorded today!

But why should the monk that appeared to Anne (see the account opposite), have given off feelings of a malevolent nature towards her? Well, if we think about it for a moment we might be able to find a possible explanation. Monks were often governed by very strict codes of conduct when it came to having anything to do with women — so much so that the merest hint of fraternization with a person of the opposite sex could result in expulsion from their order, or even worse: death. There are accounts of monks being put to death or, at the very least, severely punished and beaten because they were believed to be involved with a woman. So the monk that Ann experienced could have been showing his disapproval at the fact that a woman was sharing his 'home' and been in fear for his own safety? It would be interesting to find out if the site where Anne's house stands had any kind of connection with monks in the past.

ANNE MCAVINEY'S ACCOUNT: When I was a child my Uncle Chris loved telling me ghost stories. Some of them were basically fairytales, but others were true accounts.

The events he told me about began when he was 16, and the haunting lasted for many years until the spirit was given release. It began one day when he was digging in the back garden and found a wooden box that had been buried. Although he was curious, he was also tired and stopped for the day, deciding to investigate the box in the morning.

That night as he lay in bed he felt very restless and decided to get up and go to the toilet. As he approached the door to step onto the landing he found himself confronted by a very dark figure. This apparition was dressed in a monk's habit with the hood covering its face and shoulders. My uncle could feel a hatred and malevolence issuing from the figure and, forgetting all about the toilet, he fled into bed and lay under the covers praying for dawn.

The following morning his curiosity had diminished after his frightening encounter in the night and thinking that his ghostly visitor was in some way connected with the box that he had found the day before he hurriedly reburied it.

During the ensuing years there were pockets of activity within the house, but nothing of great importance until one night when my uncle was courting my future aunt. The house was quiet with the rest of the family out for the evening. He had decided to take my aunt to the pictures. He turned off all the lights and locked the front door. As the two of them walked down the road he turned back to look at the house and could see the living room light on. Thinking that he had perhaps forgotten to turn it off they went back.

Once again he turned the light off, locked the front door and headed back down the road with my aunt. Again he felt the urge to turn round and look at the house. This time he felt

dismay to find that the living room light was on. With not a little trepidation they went back. The house was now completely dark. My uncle put his hand on the door knob to enter the living room, but found he could not open the door. The door opens inwards and he pushed with all his might until it flew open. What confronted him then took his breath away. The living room was in complete darkness but in the centre he could see what he could only describe as a tornado with white specks swirling around. He quickly shut the door and the two of them rushed down the street. My uncle did not return until later on when he knew the rest of the family would be home. Unfortunately, they did not believe what my uncle had endured and put it down to his imagination. However, my Aunt Grace said that the events were definitely true – as I was soon to be shown myself.

Many years later, after my uncle had died, my husband and I bought the old house in 1991. As soon as we moved in to decorate strange things started to happen. I remember one day when I was painting the front bedroom window. There was nothing in the bedroom apart from a lovely old-fashioned wardrobe, which I had placed in the centre of the room to enable me to decorate. I decided to stop for a while for a cup of tea and to check on our two dogs.

About half an hour later I returned upstairs to resume painting. I had left the tin of paint beside the window with the top fully on, but found it now behind the wardrobe with paint all over the floor and the lid still firmly in place. That was just the beginning...

One night my husband and I were in bed trying to sleep when we heard the most awful guttural growl coming from a walk-in cupboard. On another occasion my husband saw a picture fall of the wall. Not that unusual, you might think, but this picture was not hung in the usual way: if you wanted to remove it from the wall you had to push upwards and then outwards. He had been sitting watching the television when the picture suddenly moved up and jumped off the wall to land beside the television. I was secretly pleased, as my husband was extremely dismissive of anything paranormal, even though he had heard the growl too.

The negative energy became stronger and stronger over the next couple of years and I often found myself quite afraid to walk up or down the stairs, as I had the feeling that someone was standing where the flight rounded to continue upstairs; if I was going down-stairs I often felt that I would be pushed from behind. My husband also had a friend who did not like to be in the house alone. He stayed with us for a while, but he felt very uncomfortable because of the atmosphere. There were instances of objects moving and thumps and bangs — all the usual phenomena of spirit energy and it all seemed to happen when I was around. The feeling that I was not welcome within my own home became stronger and stronger and the energy was building up — I could just about taste it.

One night, a few years later, my husband was out and I was in the house alone. I can't remember what I was doing at the time, but I was probably reading a book. I was quite settled until I saw a man in monk's robes standing and watching me from the kitchen doorway. He was there and then he was gone. I realized at that moment that this being had been growing stronger and stronger over the years until he had the energy to manifest himself — he had been feeding on my fear.

Around about this time new neighbours moved into our road and I soon came to know one of them, and she turned out to be a medium. I told her very little of my thoughts about the spirit who was haunting my house, as I wanted her to tell me what she picked up. She duly came to the house and told me she could feel the presence of a monk from many, many years ago. She continued to tell me that he stood on the stairs where they cornered — exactly where I had picked up on him — and that he could be felt all over the house. She visited a couple of times to clear the house of this monk, who she said was a dark spirit. He did not like me in the house and he was absolutely furious when my neighbour arrived to deal with him. She warned me that sometimes in clearances the phenomena could actually get worse instead of better, as the spirit person does not always move over to their proper place the first time. I must say though that the monk did leave and there was a warmth about the house after his departure. I only hope that he is now in a good place and has progressed as every soul should.

Since I was a child I have seen spirit people on numerous occasions and I have always believed in the spirit life. My friend who cleared the house saw that I could work in a psychic way and it is thanks to her and the teachers that followed that I became a medium doing private sittings, working in spiritualist churches and also clearing houses of energies that belong in their proper place. I like to term this 'rescue work', as you are not only helping the physical people who are often very frightened, but you are also helping the spirit person to move on into a (hopefully) better place for their soul's progression. I love my work with the spirits and I also thank the malevolent monk for showing me what fear feels like as it is through this understanding that I find I am able to comprehend the fears of other people.

There are still spirit phenomena within my house from time to time, but I welcome these events as I know my friends and loved ones are just making their presence known to me when I need them.

Sometimes a spirit person will even come to me for help. It's a funny old world.

Stuart Edmunds – Lion Hotel Experience

The next incident comes from one of the members of my investigation team: Stuart Edmunds. In addition to accompanying me on investigations, Stuart also conducts his own research into the world of ghosts and the paranormal, and is predominantly based in and around Shropshire, England.

Stuart has conducted a number of investigations at Tutbury Castle, Staffordshire (see pages 73–77), and he has captured some very interesting and thought-provoking images during his visits there. He has many incidents that are worthy of inclusion, but selected the one that follows overleaf, as he it has left a lasting and memorable impression on him.

This account once again indicates that hotels are some of the best locations at which to conduct an investigation. Stuart continues to be captivated by the world of the paranormal and his search continues for solid proof of the existence of ghosts.

STUART EDMUNDS' ACCOUNT I had been investigating several locations in Shropshire over a period of about a year, but had not actually experienced any paranormal activity first hand. However, the night that I spent at the Lion Hotel proved to be a very interesting experience.

I had investigated several paranormal hotspots and had already succeeded in catching a number of small orbs on camera. However, it was the cellar – an area of the hotel that was not usually associated with ghosts – that caught my attention. The atmosphere of this room, with all of its passageways leading off into the darkness, seemed the ideal location to uncover visual evidence of ghosts.

Despite the fact that the cellar was isolated from the rest of the hotel, I chose to spend an hour alone in the room at midnight, armed only with a night-vision camcorder and digital camera. There were a number of lights on for safety issues, so the main body of the cellar felt comfortable. However, the passageways behind me felt slightly sinister. Every few seconds, I felt a surge of cold air blowing from one passage so I checked with my torch at regular intervals to make sure that there was no one playing tricks.

Nothing out of the ordinary occurred for the first few minutes, and I began to relax as I was starting to prefer the idea of not actually witnessing anything paranormal, because of my isolation from the other members of my team! Despite this, I ventured around the whole of cellar where there were no other people and nothing to cause alarm. Feeling braver, I decided to walk up one of the unlit tunnels and here the atmosphere became slightly more interesting. Although I have visited other supposedly haunted locations, it was still very hard to force myself to walk onwards into the dark for fear of something unexpected appearing in front of me.

But it wasn't the tunnel I should have feared. As I neared the end of the passageway and started to think that nothing much was likely to happen, there was a sudden almighty bang from somewhere towards the cellar area directly behind me.

Immediately I turned and ran back along the tunnel in an attempt to find out what had caused the noise. Set into the ceiling of the cellar was a trapdoor, which had been used to access the cellar before stairs were installed. I was shocked to find that the trapdoor was vibrating. I quickly scanned the cellar for explanations, but there was nothing down there that could have caused the door to bang.

Although I was due to spend a full hour in the cellar, I decided to leave after 20 minutes. It was just as I was walking away from the trapdoor that I got the fright of my life. Suddenly, there was another almighty bang, coming straight from the trapdoor.

I turned to see the door moving as though somebody was walking on it. And so I ran upstairs to look at it from above. I discovered that the door actually came out to a bricked off space that was no longer accessible. Nobody would have been able to cause the bangs that I had heard.

Something strange also happened in the bar of the hotel, where we had succeeded in picking up a few orbs hovering above a particular seat.

Having spent an unsuccessful hour in the bar we walked out into the reception area, when my girlfriend suddenly grabbed my arm and claimed to have seen a man seated on the leather stool where we had just been photographing some orbs.

I ran back in to check the stool and four imprints on it as if someone had just got up from the stool. As I watched, the imprints began to fade.

Unfortunately, whoever had been there failed to show up again that evening.

Andrew Alden – Ghostly Visitors And Other Incidents

The final report in this section comes from Andrew Alden, who had some strange experiences when he moved house with his parents to Wales. His account is detailed over the page.

I once met Andrew when I was invited to a charity event that he had organized and I have to admit that he is certainly not the kind of person you would expect to jump to conclusions, especially where incidents of a paranormal nature are concerned.

Andrew's experiences seem to have begun at an early age indeed. From his first paranormal encounter at the tender age of four, his interest in the field has led him to conduct numerous investigations, and he continues his quest to this day.

The fascinating collection of stories detailed in this section is just the tip of an ever-increasing iceberg as far as paranormal experiences are concerned. There are many more waiting to be told.

Q&A: ANDREW ALDEN

I asked Andrew the same questions that I had asked the previous contributors:

How old were you when the apparent paranormal experience occurred and where were you?
Aged four in our house in Wales.

Were you, to the best of your knowledge, going through any stressful, emotional or psychological events at the time of the incident?
As I was young I would say that I was not experiencing any stress, psychological or emotional strain at the time. I was just a happy child, playing football and pretending to be somebody from the television.

Did you believe in the paranormal, ghosts and hauntings prior to the incident?
I am a firm believer that there is life after death and that a building can hold emotions from past experiences in the property. I take an open-minded view on hauntings and the paranormal. I will investigate and look at everyone's experiences before making a decision as to whether a property is haunted.

I base my investigations on the following philosophy: 'When you have eliminated all which is impossible, then whatever remains, however improbable, must be the truth.'

And after the experience, what are your beliefs?
As I mentioned above I am a believer in life after death and love investigating properties across Britain. Having worked with you [Phil Whyman], Ian Lawman [a medium] and other established names in the paranormal world, I have learnt and experienced many incidents that I cannot explain. I guess the only way we will ever know is when we too pass over to the other side – and God help any investigators who come across my spirit, as I'll be sure to give them a good fright!

Have you ever taken part in a séance or ouija board session?
I have taken part in many ouija board and séance sessions. I sway more to séances, as they seem to evoke more feelings, emotions and experiences, than the ouija board.

I have observed ouija board sessions and then asked all involved to close their eyes and it usually spells a load of rubbish, but on occasions it has spelled out dates and names. Maybe some spirits need to see through our eyes to be able to communicate and others don't. Could it be due to different planes of the spirit world? I would not suggest to any one to take part in ouija boards sessions without a medium present to control it.

ANDREW ALDEN'S ACCOUNT: I saw my first spirit at the age of four, but the one I wish to tell you about was witnessed when I was about seven or eight years of age. We moved from Derbyshire to Porthcawl in South Wales. The house we moved into was a late-Victorian detached property just a few minutes walk to the sea. One day, when we had been living in the property for a few months, my brother, sister and I saw two brass ornamental ash-trays floating in the air in the living room. They were suspended at about waist-height and they placed themselves on the floor next to the sofa as if someone was sitting on the sofa having a cigarette. I didn't smell any smoke.

My mother noticed they had moved when she came into the room and became quite hysterical. She refused to enter to room until my father returned from the business trip he was on.

Many strange and unexplained things occurred to me while I was living in that house. I saw three apparitions — two women and a man. The man stood looking at me while I was in bed and one of the women did the same, although I also saw her at my bedroom window looking out over the backyard. I saw the other woman at the bottom of the stairs — she looked at me but gave no acknowledgment and walked through the closed living room door. I also felt myself being touched while turning on the bedroom light and objects disappeared, some of which have never been found. My mother also recalls having her bedclothes pulled off her as she slept.

The majority of the incidents in this house happened to me, although a few happened to my mother. The only incident that my brother and sister witnessed was the ashtray incident.

I currently live in York, but my experiences in Wales led me to investigate and study the paranormal a great deal in the years to come and I am now a paranormal investigator.

A medium confirmed that I was sensitive to spirits and having told him about the incidents I've described, he felt that the spirits targeted me because of my sensitivity.

Years after leaving the Welsh property I found out that a previous owner had lost two husbands in the house (both from heart attacks); one had died in the shed and the other in the backyard. Could the lady looking from my bedroom window have been the grieving wife?

10

My Top 10 Favourite Haunted Places

I'm often asked what my favourite haunted locations are and where I would like to conduct a paranormal investigation, given the opportunity. There are many fantastic and fascinating buildings and locations around Britain that promise paranormal experiences, so compiling a section detailing my favourite sites was always going to a difficult task. However, here are 10 of my favourite locations, some of which I've investigated, while others remain on my wish list.

10 THE RED LION INN
Avebury, Wiltshire, England

I have conducted at least three paranormal investigations at the Red Lion over the past few years. The building is believed to date from the 17th century and served as a domestic dwelling until it became a coaching inn at the beginning of the 19th century.

The most prominent ghost to reside at the Red Lion Inn is Florrie, the unfortunate wife of an extremely jealous husband. The events surrounding her untimely demise date back to the time of the English Civil War, when Florrie took it upon herself to engage in some extra-marital activities while her husband was away fighting. But alas, Florrie's timing was impeccably bad – so much so that her husband caught her red-handed with her paramour.

One gunshot later and the wayward wife's hot-blooded lover was stone dead, with Florrie following soon after. Legend has it that with a swift flick of the wrist, Florrie's throat was slit from ear-to-ear. Just to make absolutely certain of her demise, her husband unceremoniously dumped her body down the well that can still be seen in the inn's lounge. And her husband hadn't finished there – he went on to drop a huge boulder on top of her body to make sure she stayed where she was! Personally, I think that slitting her throat would have sufficed, don't you? The unfortunate Florrie haunts the Red Lion Inn to this day.

Other ghostly forms that are said to roam the inn include the spirits of two young children. They are said to look frightened and are most frequently seen in the 'Avenue' bedroom. Sometimes the two small ghosts are accompanied by an uncaring woman, who ignores their snivelling and sorrowful faces.

PREVIOUS: *Like the ruin seen here at Tutbury Castle, which is in fact a man-made folly, nothing appears quite what it seems in the paranormal world!*

BELOW: *The infamous Red Lion Inn in Wiltshire. Legend has it that the well that is situated inside is the final resting place for the unfortunate Florrie.*

LEFT: *Woodchester Mansion, occupying the Number Nine spot in my Top 10. See the investigation report for further information on this location.*

Other odd occurrences at the Red Lion include strange light anomalies, noises and cold-spots. On one of our visits, Nick heard young children playing and laughing outside – at about 2 am!

When this incident was investigated further there was nobody to be seen. On another investigation, Nick and another team member saw a grey shape move across the upper landing and disappear through a wall.

If you get the chance, a visit to the Red Lion is recommended. You can even stay the night in one of the haunted rooms – if you dare!

9 WOODCHESTER MANSION
Gloucestershire, England

Woodchester Mansion in Gloucestershire is one of the most impressive sights I have ever seen. Dating from the 1850s, this incomplete stone building is surrounded by a strange air that almost every visitor senses upon arrival.

Nestled in a valley and situated at the end of a long driveway that is almost a mile long, Woodchester Mansion seems to stare straight at you – something that is perhaps due to the gargoyles precariously perched around its roofline. Inside, the building is a sprawling mix of rooms and corridors, set out over several floors. The mansion also has a chapel with lead-lined stained-glass windows. The drawing room is perhaps the most striking of all of its rooms, with a vaulted ceiling and bay windows. Built by William Leigh, Woodchester Mansion's incomplete state is something of a mystery and many rumours persist as to why it was left in this way. Even the workmen's tools were left where they had been at the time the building was abandoned.

Did workers leave the site because of stories that Woodchester Mansion was haunted? Or is there a more down-to-earth explanation for the apparently sudden desertion of the building? Either way, one thing does seem to be clear from the numerous incidents that have been reported over the years – Woodchester certainly its fair share of ghosts!

Paranormal activity at the location includes the ghostly forms of soldiers in the mansion and around the grounds (the Canadian and American military set up camp at Woodchester in World War Two, using parts of the building for storage); a dwarf-like figure; a Roman Centurion, who haunts the driveway and surrounding area; strange noises, and unexplained lights inside and outside the property, along with inexplicable smells that are said to waft through the building.

Woodchester Mansion is open to the public, so a visit is a *must* if you are in the vicinity.

8 CASTLE RISING CASTLE
Norfolk, England

Castle Rising is a location where I've always wanted to spend the night. Dating back to the 1100s, the site is home to one of Britain's most extensive sets of ruins. Its impressive form was once the residence of a rather sinister character – Queen Isabella, who was nicknamed the 'She-wolf of France'. Isabella was more than likely party to the gruesome murder of her unfortunate husband Edward II. In the years that followed this awful event Queen Isabella apparently went slowly insane. People have reported hearing her crazed and maniacal shrieks on occasion – could this be a throwback to murderous times, perhaps?

7 THE GALLERIES OF JUSTICE
Nottingham, England

The Galleries of Justice has to be one of my all-time favourite locations and I have held several overnight investigations here in what is my home city.

Dating back to the 1700s and formerly the site of the City Hall, the Galleries of Justice was one of the few locations in England where, depending on your crime, you could have been tried, convicted, imprisoned and put to death within the same building. Many criminals were hanged on the front steps, where the main entrance to the building is now located. Those who were lucky enough to escape the hangman's noose often found themselves shipped off to Australia, where a life of hard labour at a penal colony awaited them.

Many a devious and murderous villain entered this building never to know freedom again and there are people convinced that some of these miscreants still lurk within the shadows of the building.

Specific sites inside the Galleries of Justice that are reputedly haunted include the Courtroom, where a dark, unidentified figure has been seen looking down from the public viewing area; the Bath-house, which is situated on one of the lower levels and where strange noises have been heard and objects have been moved by invisible hands; and the Night Cell, which tends to be a particular favourite with

paranormal investigators, because in this location feelings of oppression seem to wash over you for no apparent reason. The Entrance Hall is yet another haunted area, where an old man has sometimes been seen. Add all of this to the numerous unexplained light anomalies, noises and smells that have been experienced here and you have a very interesting location indeed.

So who exactly is behind the hauntings and activities that occur at the Galleries of Justice? Well, according to the many psychics who have investigated the location, there is one individual whose name just keeps popping up – William Saville. This unsavoury individual murdered his entire family before being put to death, thus condemning him to wander the corridors and rooms of the Galleries for evermore. Some people believe he is responsible for many of the phenomena witnessed here, but who knows?

During one of my investigations at the Galleries of Justice, a mysterious hooded figure was seen moving around the back of the main courtroom by several different team members. Numerous unexplained noises have also been heard, and cold spots have been experienced frequently. Nottingham's Galleries of Justice are open to the general public, so do visit the site – but prepare to be spooked.

OPPOSITE: *Comprising one of the largest sets of ruins in the British Isles, Castle Rising Castle still echoes with the cries of 'Mad' Queen Isabella.*

ABOVE: *The Galleries of Justice, Nottingham. One of the most haunted buildings in England, and where a dark-hooded figure was seen by several investigators in one of the courtrooms.*

6 CHILLINGHAM CASTLE
Chillingham, Northumberland, England

Chillingham Castle is a location at which I have long wanted to conduct a paranormal investigation in the hope of acquainting myself with the castle's many spectral occupants. Dating back to the 12th century, Chillingham

ABOVE: *Chillingham Castle, Northumberland. One location in which I would like to hold an investigation.*

has seen some notable and distinguished visitors pass through its doors, including Henry III and Edward I. Its cold, stone exterior is a formidable sight and is enough in itself to give visitors goosebumps.

The most famous of Chillingham's ghostly lodgers is the 'Radiant Boy'. His particular haunt of preference is the castle's Pink Room, where his pitiful cries have been heard and his frail form seen, dressed in blue clothing. The fragile bones of a young child have actually been discovered behind one of the interior walls of the castle. Could these be the last remains of the 'Radiant Boy', and if so why was he walled up here?

Another of Chillingham's ghosts is the forlorn Lady Berkeley, who was the wife of one Lord Grey, until he ran away with the good lady's sister leaving her, quite literally, holding the baby. Lady Berkeley's form has been seen

roaming the castle's many corridors late at night, much to the horror of witnesses.

Other strange phenomena that have been experienced at Chillingham Castle include light anomalies, cold spots, unexplained noises, objects moving and inexplicable smells. For those of you who would like to experience the spooky goings-on at Chillingham Castle, why not book a room for a couple of nights and see if you encounter any things that go bump in the night?

5 BODELWYDDAN CASTLE
Denbighshire, Wales

Bodelwyddan Castle (pronounced 'Bodel-withan') is a grand, atmospheric site, especially when viewed under a starlit night sky. Parts of the castle date from the 1400s and the building originally started life as a manor house,

although it is believed that an even older property was once situated on the very same site. In 1829, while the building was being renovated, human bones were discovered within one of the castle's walls. If you think that was odd, it is believed that they were actually put back into the wall and covered over again where they remain to this day...

Could the presence of these bones be connected to the amount of spirit activity occurring at Bodelwyddan Castle? There have been many ghostly happenings reported at the castle over the past few years, which is hardly surprising considering the plethora of phantoms said to be roaming about there.

In the castle's Sculpture Gallery the shadowy figure of a woman has been seen on several occasions. In another of the castle's galleries, the figure of a soldier has been witnessed – Bodelwyddan was used as an officers' mess and place of recuperation during World War One. In the Terrace Tea Room, the apparition of a 'blue' lady has been

ABOVE: Beautiful Bodelwyddan Castle, where the sad form of a spectral soldier roams – just one of the numerous ghosts that have been reported here.

reported. Alongside these three named ghosts, several other unidentified, shadowy figures have been seen around the castle. Couple these sightings with numerous incidents of unexplained noises and light anomalies and you have a great location in which to conduct a paranormal investigation.

4 LEAP CASTLE
County Offaly, Ireland

Leap Castle (pronounced 'Lep') has a reputation as one of the most paranormally active castles in the world, and with such a bloody and violent history it's little wonder!

Built in the 14th and 15th centuries, it was originally used to guard the surrounding area and serve as a deterrent for anybody who had ideas about entering Munster via the Slieve Bloom pass. The castle was initially owned by the O'Bannon clan, but later inhabited by the O'Carrolls. It served as a formidable prison for the clan's unfortunate captives during times of war.

The castle eventually passed over to the Darby family, descendants of whom are said to be responsible for the most famous – or infamous – of the castle's paranormal characters: the 'Elemental'.

Hundreds of years ago, in the area of the castle that is now known as the Bloody Chapel, a truly gruesome and brutal murder occurred. At that time the O'Carrolls were falling out with each other left, right and centre, and none of the family members knew who they could trust elsewhere within the clan. One day, while one of the O'Carroll brothers – a priest – was conducting mass for family, a rival sibling stormed into the chapel, driving his sword deep into his brother's body. The fatally wounded priest fell across the altar, eventually bleeding to death.

This blasphemous act combined with the rest of Leap Castle's dark and deadly history left an ever-present air of evil within its ancient walls. You get a very real idea of the castle's turbulent history when you step back in time to the very beginning of the 1900s, when several workmen were called in to clear out the castle's Oubliette (from the French *oublier*, meaning 'to forget'), a little drop-floor room with only one access point. To their absolute horror they found the place full of bones – they eventually disposed of three cartloads in all.

The prisoners would have been thrown into this 'place of forgetting' and if they didn't become impaled on the vicious spike rising from the floor, they would have died a slow,

BELOW: *Leap Castle, where murder and feuding were once rife, and where the disturbing entity known as the Elemental made its presence known to Mrs Darby – big time!*

painful death from starvation, while the smell of cooking drifted through the castle.

The Elemental, the castle's most talked-about spirit, is described as being the size of a sheep, with black, sunken eyes set within an inhuman face. The creature is accompanied by the stench of rotting meat. The vile Elemental is believed to have been conjured up by Mildred Darby, who practiced the black arts – Leap Castle has regretted her actions ever since. Other strange phenomena that have been experienced at the site include strange lights, which were witnessed when the castle was locked up and unoccupied, and unexplained noises and smells. There have even been reports of freak accidents occurring at the castle.

For the moment however, the spirits within Leap are content to live alongside the castle's present occupants.

3 THE EDINBURGH VAULTS
Edinburgh, Scotland

One place where I have been lucky to conduct several investigations is the Edinburgh Vaults (see pages 58–63 and 78–81). Dating back to 1785, the site consists of 19 arches that form part of the city's South Bridge. All manner of businesses and dwellings were situated in the vaults. However, activities at the site went unchecked and the vaults soon became a dingy, dark and foreboding place – the scene of many a mugging, assault and murder.

Eventually the Edinburgh Vaults were more or less abandoned. They were filled in and forgotten, with the dark secrets they had witnessed sealed up. In 1980 they were rediscovered, an event that many individuals believe sparked off the now-familiar ghostly activity within.

The Edinburgh Vaults are the frequent haunt of the infamous Mr Boots, said to be a nasty man of stocky stature, and a little boy called Jack. Along with a small, scruffy-looking dog these two individuals are the most commonly reported ghostly inhabitants at the location.

Other incidents that have been reported here include items of clothing being pulled; hair being tugged; both cold and hot spots; light anomalies and strange feelings of sadness and anger.

The Edinburgh Vaults are open to visitors and there are guided tours so that you can experience first-hand the atmosphere of one of Scotland's most haunted locations.

2 THE TOWER OF LONDON
London, England

The Tower of London is without a doubt one of the most paranormally active buildings in the world. It is a site at which I would love to hold a paranormal investigation. For me the attraction is not just paranormal, as I love old buildings with long and intricate histories. However, I am not going to go into huge detail about the Tower's history here, as the building has too immense and fascinating a past to be covered in detail here.

Built in 1078 by William the Conqueror, the Tower of London is one of the most recognizable of buildings and is the home of countless spirits. Henry VI, murdered here in the 1400s, is said to haunt the castle. He is an 'anniversary' ghost, appearing annually on the date he was killed, May 21, 1471. A 'white lady' haunts the oldest part of the Tower and is said to leave a strong scent of perfume whenever she is present. The unfortunate figures of Lady Jane Grey and the Anne Boleyn are said to frequent the area known as Tower Green. The ghosts of two children, believed to be Princes Edward and Richard, are believed to haunt the Bloody Tower – rumour having it that their uncle, Richard III, in his quest for the throne, secreted their remains within the grounds. They have been seen on occasion playing and running through the grounds. And, in the mid-17th century, the skeletons of two young boys were found buried beneath the staircase of the White Tower. Could these have been the two princes?

But with the Tower of London occupying second place in my top 10, what could possibly be my number one paranormal site?

1 BORLEY RECTORY
Borley, Essex, England

Borley Rectory has to be my first choice without a doubt. It is a truly enigmatic location, one that I have grown up with, and one that I used to daydream about visiting so that I could experience the various phenomena that have occured within it for myself.

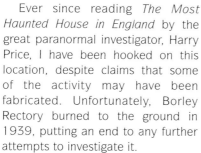

Ever since reading *The Most Haunted House in England* by the great paranormal investigator, Harry Price, I have been hooked on this location, despite claims that some of the activity may have been fabricated. Unfortunately, Borley Rectory burned to the ground in 1939, putting an end to any further attempts to investigate it.

The most infamous of Borley's ghosts was that of a spectral nun, who was often seen in the garden, she was seen so frequently that the route she used became known as 'Nun's Walk'. On some occasions, dinner guests were alarmed to find her gaunt image staring at them from outside. According to information received during a séance, the nun, who was French and went by the name of Marie-Lairre, was apparently strangled to death before being interred in the cellar.

Borley's Rectory was a hot-bed of poltergeist activity, with all manner of objects taking flight and being moved by unseen forces. Harry Price himself was almost struck on several occasions by such airborne paraphernalia. Footsteps were often heard coming from the vicinity of unoccupied rooms, incoherent voices were heard, and several times the sound of a woman's voice shattered the eerie silence, screaming the words, 'Don't Carlos, don't!' Add to all this the ethereal phantom coach and horses, which careered through the property and out via the front lawn, and you had a very interesting location indeed.

Matters really began to heat up when Lionel Foyster and his family took over at Borley. The first thing that happened was that his wife, Marianne, was viciously hit in the face (she went on to become the focus for much of the paranormal activity that occurred during their tenancy).

Things continued to go missing, only to subsequently reappear in completely different places and the paranormal activity intensified over time. The strangest of the phenomena to occur at Borley Rectory was a series of messages scrawled across the walls. Addressed to Marianne, they often pleaded to her for help. These missives continued to appear for some time, although their source was never properly identified.

During a séance the fate of the Rectory was foretold by a spirit calling himself Sunex Amures. He revealed that, along with several other spirits, he would set the building alight and raze the place to the ground.

This turned out to be a false prediction, as the building did not burn down on the date given by Sunex Amures. However, Borley Rectory did indeed burn to the ground in 1939. The official account is that a paraffin lamp had been accidentally knocked over, setting the place alight, although rumours circulated that the fire was the result of an insurance scam.

Nowadays, the site of Borley Rectory is occupied by houses. I believe that one of the original buildings – an outbuilding – still exists to this day, as does the original quaint, but creepy, church, where unexplained happenings are still reported to take place! So there you have it – my Number One haunted location. There are numerous good publications detailing the ghostly goings-on at Borley Rectory (see 'Further Reading' on page 125).

OPPOSITE: *Occupying the Number One spot in my Top 10, Borley Rectory has fascinated me since I was a youngster and I would have dearly loved to have spent the night here. Alas, the place burned down under mysterious circumstances in 1939, although Borley's church still remains, and is also reputedly haunted.*

PARANORMAL INVESTIGATION QUESTIONNAIRE

I have included here a simple set of questions that you may find useful during witness interviews. You may wish to use them in your own form and print them off.

1. Witness name:
_____

2. Contact details:
_____

3. What were your religious beliefs?
_____

4. What are they now?
_____

5. Were you on any medication at the time of the experience?
_____

6. Were you, to the best of your knowledge, going through any stressful, emotional or psychological event at the time of the experience?
_____
_____

7. Had you been drinking alcohol at the time?
_____

8. What was the approximate date and time of the experience?
_____

9. Describe the experience in as much detail as possible (noises, smells, sensations etc.):
_____
_____
_____

10. Did you believe in the paranormal, ghosts or hauntings prior to the experience?
_____
_____
_____

11. And after the experience, what are your beliefs?
_____
_____
_____
_____

12. Have you ever been involved in a ouija board session?
_____
_____

13. If so, when?
_____
_____

14. What happened, if anything?
_____
_____
_____
_____

15. Please give the names of any other witnesses who have had similar experiences at the location in question:
_____
_____
_____
_____
_____

FURTHER READING

Here is a list of publications that you may find of interest should you wish to explore the realm of ghosts and the paranormal further. Some of the publications may be a little hard to source, but are well worth the effort of doing so.

Richard Jones
Haunted Britain and Ireland
(New Holland)

Richard Jones
Haunted Inns of Britain and Ireland
(New Holland)

John Brooks
The Good Ghost Guide
(Jarrold Publishing)

John and Anne Spencer
The Encyclopedia of Ghosts and Spirits
(Headline)

John and Anne Spencer
The Encyclopedia of Ghosts and Spirits Vol. 2
(Headline)

Harry Price
The Most Haunted House in England
(Longman Green)

Ivan Banks
The Enigma of Borley Rectory
(Foulsham)

Alasdair Alpin MacGregor
The Ghost Book: Strange Hauntings in Britain
(Robert Hale)

Simon Marsden
The Haunted Realm
(Little, Brown)

John Mason
Haunted Heritage
(Collins and Brown)

INDEX

PICTURE ACKNOWLEDGEMENTS

All photographs taken by Phil Whyman, apart from:

Stuart Edmunds (pages 1, 16, 18, 107)

John Mason (pages 10, 116, 119)

Simon Deacon, Steve Griffiths & Swadlincote Paranormal Investigations (page 19)

Duncan Soar (page 39)

Dave Wharmby (page 41)

Nick Scrimshaw & Dead Haunted Nights (page 72)

Steven Nettleship (page 85)

Chris Thomas (page 90)

Hannah Blake (page 96)

Gareth Jones (page 110)

Topfoto/Charles Walker (page 121)

Alan Marshall (page 125)

Gülen Shevki-Taylor (page 128)

ACKNOWLEDGEMENTS

As you would imagine when undertaking a project like this, there have been numerous people who have helped me along the way to its completion.

First and foremost I would like to thank Charlotte-Victoria Drew, for her endless support and belief in me, for spurring me into action when needed and keeping me sane; I don't think I would have completed this project so readily without her.

The same thanks also go to my mum, dad and sister for their continued support.

Gratitude goes to my friend, Nick Scrimshaw, whose hard work during and outside of investigations was invaluable – thank you. I would also like to thank the fearless Vince Draper, for his generosity in helping me with investigations: does nothing scare this man?

My appreciation also goes out to Chris Fryer, for his help on investigations (especially the driving to and fro, and his occasional snoring!).

To all the people who contributed their personal experiences, without which this book would have been incomplete, a big thank-you.

Thanks to my old mate Richard Jones ('Jonesy'), whose books I have a great fondness for and in which I have found many an interesting story. Thanks also for the conversation – even if it's usually after midnight!

To my charming friend Leslie Smith at Tutbury Castle, who has always welcomed me and my team, I thank you. Warmest thanks to Dave Wharmby – may you continue to be a success. Thanks to: Chris 'the dude' Thomas, Simon Deacon, Stuart Edmunds, Steve Griffiths, Trevor (at the Galleries of Justice, Nottingham).

My appreciation goes to the owners, managers and custodians of the locations I have featured and investigated.

And many thanks to all those people who continue to support me and email their kind words and messages. I am very touched and flattered, thank you.